LOVE IS LOVE

THE ABSOLUTE MUST-HAVE GUIDE TO COMING OUT
FROM YOUR FAVOURITE AGONY UNCLES

LOVE IS LOVE

**MATTHEW MACKINNON
AND RYAN PAYNE**

THREAD

Published by Thread in 2023

An imprint of Storyfire Ltd.
Carmelite House
50 Victoria Embankment
London EC4Y 0DZ

www.thread-books.com

Copyright © Matthew Mackinnon and Ryan Payne, 2023

Matthew Mackinnon and Ryan Payne have asserted their right to be identified as the author of this work.

All rights reserved. No part of this publication may be reproduced, stored in any retrieval system, or transmitted, in any form or by any means, electronic, mechanical, photocopying, recording or otherwise, without the prior written permission of the publishers.

Cover photograph by Joe Hawk Murphy, © 2023 The River Group

Some names have been changed to protect the identity and privacy of those who have contributed to this book.

ISBN: 978-1-83790-038-1
eBook ISBN: 978-1-83790-037-4

To anyone who feels like they don't fit in because they're different. This is for you. You are safe and welcome here.

To our family, friends and online community we have built who made us feel safe and welcomed, we adore and thank YOU for accepting us, motivating us and simply all heartedly loving us.

CONTENTS

Love Is Love 9

Introduction: Love Is Love 11
Chapter 1: Discovering You Are 'Different' 19
Chapter 2: What's a Pronoun? 54
Chapter 3: Coming Out 85
Chapter 4: Living with Pride 122
Chapter 5: Mental Health 147
Chapter 6: How to Beat the Bullies! 159
Chapter 7: For the Parents 168
Chapter 8: Love Is Love 198

Letters to Ourselves 209
A Letter from Matthew and Ryan 215
Resources 217
Acknowledgements 222

Love Is Love

Matthew and Ryan are popular LGBTQIA+ creators who share their life of love and adventure with their online family of seven million followers. They lead busy dynamic lives, creating a wide variety of content from travel to comedy and sharing it with their loyal online family. Their main goal is to make people smile, one piece of content at a time.

Matthew is a gentle, kind-hearted soul who is everyone's friend and has a mischievous appetite for pranks, particularly when his fiery partner is the target of them.

Ryan is warm-hearted, generous and welcoming. He usually jumps before he thinks and is always ready to support anyone and everyone he can.

As individuals, they are like chalk and cheese but, aside from their love for food, there is one big thing they have in common.

They love each other and they love sharing it with the world!

Love Is Love is their roadmap to being your authentic self. This is the ultimate guidebook to growing up LGBTQIA+.

INTRODUCTION
Love Is Love

The Matthew and Ryan story started when we met, on Tinder, in the autumn of 2015. Our early romance was far from straightforward!

Matthew: I really liked Ryan but was nervous about getting involved with someone, so I kept putting him off when he suggested we meet up. After a couple of weeks, I finally felt ready, so I rang him and asked him if he wanted to do my make-up for Halloween.

Ryan: I really liked Matthew, but he kept rejecting me. We stopped texting for a while, but then, after pieing me off for two weeks, he rang me out of the blue and asked me to do his make-up. I was like, jog on. Goodbye. Delete.

Matthew: But I did *really* like him! So I turned up at the nightclub where he was working on Halloween night. I was dressed as a Fab ice lolly, covered in jam and sprinkles. I don't know *what* I was thinking! I love Fab ice lollies, so my dress up was inspired by one, hoping Ryan would love them too!

Ryan: I went on my break and Matthew is standing there with hundreds and thousands stuck all over his face! He was trying to talk to me seriously, while picking sugar off his chin with his tongue. I couldn't stop laughing. That's when I saw a different side to him. He was sweet and geeky.

Matthew: Me dressed as an ice lolly. That was how our love story began.

Ryan: On our first date, Matthew picked me up in his very own car. Not gonna lie, I thought he was just the coolest – I was a university student and he just seemed so grown up!

Matthew: I took Ryan to Mayflower Park where there were fireworks, snacks and fairground rides, right out of a romantic movie. It was a perfect day.

Ryan: Matthew asked a lot of questions and he was a great gentleman, our conversation was just effortless. It was such a great date, and it was then that I knew there was more to our relationship than simply being friends and that, ultimately, there could be something really special between us.

#MatthewandRyan as a content creator brand was more straightforward.

Ryan already had a YouTube channel when we met, and soon after we got together we started creating. Our first ever video was of a trip to London, and we were only recording ourselves so we could look back on our first holiday together. But we soon discovered a love of filming and creating content. After

Matthew took part in the 'boyfriend tag' and the 'cinnamon challenge' on Ryan's old channel we decided it made sense for us to start our own channel because we just had so much fun filming together as a hobby.

When we started our Matthew and Ryan YouTube channel in the beginning of 2016, we never could have imagined the supportive and loving community that would form around us. As soon as we started documenting the special moments in our relationship we realised that there was a lack of same-gender couples on social media at that time, especially when it came to male same-gender couples who weren't all six packs, guns and hunky, which we most certainly weren't. It became our mission to start normalising this in every avenue we possibly could. For a while we tried to figure out what would work, experimenting with fashion and filters and trying to find our online selves, but by the time TikTok came along in 2018 we realised that just being ourselves – messing around, laughing, pranking and being joyful – was what we wanted to share with the world. Our first TikTok video got three million views and we haven't looked back since.

Naturally, we want to share our lives as a gay couple, but our content was and still is about having fun, playing pranks, travelling and capturing our love for each other, and our gorgeous furbaby, Roscoe. As a couple, we live together and work together, so we are very close. Our life is the same as every other young couple – dressing up for date nights, squabbling in the supermarket, driving each other crazy then making up by cuddling on the sofa with a pizza.

Except we are doing these things in public and – of course – we're both guys.

♡ We're here for you

Soon after we started posting videos of our life online, young people began to contact us telling us about the kind of problems they were experiencing in coming out. We replied and helped as best we could, and in the years since, every week countless messages flood our in-boxes from young people and their family members and friends looking for answers to *so* many questions.

- *How do I know if I am gay?*
- *My son says he is gay – is it a 'phase'?*
- *When should I come out? And how?*
- *Why should I come out at all? It's nobody else's business!*
- *Everyone was kissing at the school disco – except me!*
- *I've been outed, and I'm not ready!*
- *Friends are nice to my face then tease me for being gay online.*
- *My best friend has a crush on me!*
- *How do I deal with being bullied?*
- *My family don't accept me.*
- *Mum thinks it's a phase – what should I do?*
- *I don't know what I like. How can I figure it out?*

We know how scary, lonely and overwhelming it can be, and we are going to help you with every step of your journey. *Love Is Love* will be the comforting, supportive friend you need to help you with a process that can be deeply confusing, but ultimately very rewarding. We are here to help you:

- figure out your identity. There is so much talk about gender, sexuality and labels these days, we will help you find the 'you' you feel most comfortable with – with labels or not!
- find LOADS of practical advice on how to come out – or not. We'll help you make the choice to share however much or little information you need without feeling pressure from yourself – or anyone else
- work through some of the confusing thoughts and feelings you might have. Figuring out what you want and need can be difficult, but it's easier when you hear stories from others who have been down the same road
- look after your mental health. We have expert advice and all the resources you might need in one place
- feel confident in your own skin. We want to share ALL of our tips to help you learn how to be proud to be YOU!

This book is our roadmap for navigating and understanding LGBTQIA+ life. It's what we wish we had been given when we were discovering ourselves.

Remember: you do NOT have to go through this alone.
We are here for you – and this book contains advice, stories, encouragement and wisdom from experts and figureheads from the LGBTQIA+ community.

Mostly, this book tells OUR story: how we found ourselves – first as individuals then each other – and how, together, we built a beautiful rainbow community which we are happy to welcome you into.

It is important for us to share our stories with you because we are proud of who we are, and we want you to feel the same.

♡ Say hello to our Rainbow Tribe!

People are the most precious things to us, and we make sure that we surround ourselves with love and positivity. The relationships we have with our chosen family of friends and allies, online and off, as well as our own families are such an important part of who we are. We could not have written this book without including them.

These are the amazing humans who back us up and cheer us on. Like us, they believe that *Love Is Love*.

First up are our **Family**. Matthew's mum, dad and sister – and Ryan's dad, plus our oldest, closest friends. These are the people who have shared our lives, as individuals and as a couple, loving and supporting us from day one. We are both blessed to have family who love and accept us unconditionally. Family relationships can get complicated when you are growing up as LGBTQIA+. We've been there and are going to help you navigate your way through. Our family will be sharing their experiences of our journey through interviews and bite-sized Love Is Love Moments – where they'll be revealing a few of our secrets!

LOVE IS LOVE MOMENT:
Friends by chance

Thank God me and Ryan worked together, and he lost his phone (in the toilet) on our work night out, as we may not have been friends if he hadn't! I love them both very much, and I am very blessed to have them both in my life.

Samara, friend

Then we have our **Allies**.

Allies are the online partners and friends we have made over the years as content creators. Online and off, we have grown up together as people, creators and friends. We share content, opinions and stories with each other to make us better ambassadors for the LGBTQIA+ community. We influence each other, as well as our followers, and our allies are coming along on this journey with us – from passing on their inspirational stories to helping you make sense of this LGBTQIA+ business, just as they did with us.

We will be having revealing chats with our allies and inviting them to share their experiences and advice throughout the book.

Next – meet your **Community**.

Community are people who have come forward to share their stories to help you know you are not alone. They are out there leading happy, healthy lives as LGBTQIA+ people.

Community are the people you could become as an LGBTQIA+ person.

Our community also includes straight people, because anyone who advocates for LGBTQIA+ friends and family is an important part of our journey.

Finally – we asked the **experts**. Psychotherapist Joanna Fortune will give her insights, and Just Like Us is a brilliant charity that runs education programmes on LGBTQIA+ issues. We are so honoured to be affiliated with this brilliant organisation. Having done a School Diversity Week masterclass with them, alongside promoting their amazing work on our social media channels, we have first-hand experience of the great work Just Like Us does, and we are so grateful to them for giving us expert advice and gathering stories from their ambassadors.

Now, let's get started!

CHAPTER 1
Discovering You Are 'Different'

The most important thing for you to know right from the start is there is nothing wrong with being different. When you think about it, we are all different anyway, because no two people are the same. Everyone is unique. There is no cut-and-paste when it comes to being human.

Feeling different is difficult when we are still trying to make sense of the world around us. It is a completely normal, human reaction to want to be like everyone else. It makes complete sense to want to fit in with your family and your friends, to enjoy doing the things they do and be a full part of what is going on around you. We all need to feel we belong and so being different can feel lonely, even frightening. As you will see in our personal stories, we have both been there.

However, as we said at the start, what we both discovered is that being 'different' is *not* a bad thing. For us, celebrating the fact we are 'different' has been the key to success, in every area of our lives.

Embracing your difference could be the best thing you will ever do!

MATTHEW

'I had a great family – but I was afraid to be "me".'

Growing up, I was lucky to have a happy home life. I was very sheltered and protected from the outside world; I got on well with my family, and we were supportive of each other. My family were loving, even if we didn't seem like the most affectionate bunch – in the typical sense where people say 'I love you' on the regular – but we all knew we loved each other and made countless amazing memories together.

I knew my mum and dad loved me to bits, but I never connected the dots that they accepted me completely for who I was until later in life. We were a conventional family. We didn't know anyone who was gay within the family so the subject never came up. Looking back, I realise that the reason my family never talked about the possibility of me being gay was because it didn't matter. I was just Matthew, and they loved and accepted me for whoever I was. That was a given, so why bring it up and possibly embarrass me? I see their point, but at the time, I did feel anxious about it.

I remember once watching Dale Winton – a really camp TV personality – at a friend's house, and hearing someone comment, 'He's a poof and he's proud of it.' The person who said it clearly thought it was disgusting and they looked around to see if others agreed with them. It left me feeling scared that this would be how I would be treated if I acted like Dale Winton. It made me distance myself from people further and stopped me from talking about my personal feelings.

No one in my life was horrible to me about my campness, but at the same time no one actually spoke to me about it or made me feel openly accepted. This was especially stressful at school as it was the time when classmates probably started wondering if I was gay. I now understand that no one spoke to me about it as they didn't want to pressure me into talking about myself if I wasn't ready. I was loved and accepted so there was no problem as far as anyone else was concerned.

My family loved me. They weren't worried about what other people would think of me being gay, but it still bothered me.

It was small things like, after I turned ten, family members would often ask me that classic question: have you got a girlfriend at school? I would laugh it off, but it forced me to question why I didn't want a girlfriend. Was there something wrong with me? It would leave me feeling really confused because I would look at boys at school and think I was more attracted to them than the girls. It's a shame because looking back I feel like this should have been such a fun experience. I know that a lot of people have the same thought after coming out. You find yourself bottling everything up, regardless of what others think around you.

I always got on so well with my dad – he is so much fun! He is a prankster (that's where I get it from), and he used to take me bell ringing, which I really enjoyed. However, Dad loved football, and that was something I couldn't connect with him on. Football felt so uncomfortable to me and made me aware that I was different from all the other boys around me. I would rather sit and talk and play with the girls.

Looking back, I wish somebody had explained to me that this was okay. But I guess it was a conversation people didn't want to have back then. And maybe this is part of the reason it's so important for me now to tell my story to younger people.

I often found myself trying to make other people feel more comfortable by conforming to their ideas of 'normal' rather than just being myself, especially at school. It was exhausting. I pushed myself to do things that I didn't enjoy, like PE in school with the boys, which was often rugby or football. I hated it, and it made me stressed and angry in the run up to every lesson.

Looking back, I realise what a shame it was that I felt this way, because the fact that I was 'different' was actually an asset! People were drawn to me, and I made many friends because of it. I stood out from the crowd, and that is a good thing. What I know now, and I wish I had known then, is that that 'difference' is not something to be ashamed of. It's something to embrace and feel excited about!

RYAN

'I never knew the word gay – I was just being me.'

When I was ten years old I gave my favourite Pokémon card to a boy (although I wish I'd kept it – it would be worth a fortune now!). It was such an innocent thing to do and looking back I think it was totally adorable, but if it had happened just a couple of years later, when people around me started to date and get into relationships, it would not have been seen the same way. I reckon people would have thought it was weird, or 'gay' or seen it as me flirting with that boy. But it wasn't. I just wanted that boy to have my Pokémon card.

I also remember being young and playing kiss chase in the playground. I would always chase after the boys, which, looking back, was so cute and innocent. I had never even heard the word 'gay'.

It was only when I got older and hit puberty, and when the boys around me started to really like kissing girls and dating them, that I kind of knew I was different.

I loved dancing, and Dad used to drop me off at dance classes. He always really encouraged me. I was the only boy in the class, and I absolutely loved it! But then one week, the teacher insisted that I learn the male steps. She was adjusting my back into the 'correct' male form, and I was thinking 'No! I don't want to do this! I want to be the one spinning around!' That made me question myself. It felt awkward and uncomfortable. In the end, that incident made me drop out of my dance classes, which was a real shame.

I was only 11 or 12 when the words 'gay' and 'lesbian' started to be used in a bad way. I was quite a feminine boy growing up, so a lot of people automatically called me gay. That label always stayed with me, even though I didn't come out until a lot later in my life.

It was around then that things started getting harder for me in school. The school environment can be quite tough when you're trying to deal with your sexuality; people can be bullies.

When I was older, I started doing a hairdressing course. Me and three other boys would attend this class on a Tuesday instead of going to school. My dad encouraged me and said I could open a barber shop one day! But people in school were awful to us. They would bully us, saying things like, 'You're doing hairdressing – you're gay!' The negative connotation was so intense I found it traumatic. It actually put me off hairdressing, which was something that I loved.

People using 'gay' as a derogatory term has really stuck with me. But it also felt like they were just slapping a label on me for the way I was when, actually, I was just being me. I think it's why I don't really like 'labels'. It's not nice to have others identify you before you are ready to identify yourself. Yes, I am gay, but first and foremost, I am an individual. Me.

But I suppose that is also why I am proud to identify as 'different' now. It wasn't easy when I was in school, but today I understand that being different is a gift because it means that you stand out. If I wasn't different, I wouldn't shine as brightly as I do today.

♡ How do I know 'what' or 'who' I am?

It's so great that conversations have opened up about LGBTQIA+ identities but – full disclosure – we think it's actually more challenging to figure out who you are in today's society than it was for us, because there are so many more labels for people to identify with and so much more information to consume!

So, we are going to try and break it down for you. Sexuality is a very personal thing – between you, your body, your mind and your heart. And it usually starts with… The Crush!

♡ Does a same-gender crush mean I'm not straight?

Most people, at least once in their lifetime, will have an attraction to someone of the same gender, but this doesn't necessarily mean anything.

The world is full of beautiful people, and sometimes we are just attracted to good looks, regardless of gender. We are gay men, and we still look at women and think they are *gorgeous* – even though we might not fancy them.

You might be a boy and admire a man's physical shape or simply their stunning smile – but that does not mean you aren't straight. It's important not to jump to conclusions and send yourself into a panic spiral. There are no rules, and there is no right or wrong way when it comes to who you are attracted or not attracted to. Crushes are our first indication that we are becoming romantic, sexual beings. Same-gender crushes might pass or grow. Maybe you don't have any crushes at all, which can also make you feel left out. The important thing is to relax and enjoy your feelings of attraction and friendship, and not worry about what they mean. There is no right or wrong way when it comes to who you are attracted to.

♡ Explore different things

Although there seemed to be fewer labels, it was still hard when we were coming out (a million years ago – OLD guys!), simply because there weren't the same number of online spaces for young people to explore and meet up with each other. Honestly, if we had been able to use the social media networks that are here today, our lives would possibly have been much easier. It's really something you can take advantage of and while you do it, be open to exploring different things. Reach out to and chat with people (safely!), look around you and explore the different worlds that are open to you. Follow people you like, and comment on threads if you feel comfortable. Learning about your sexual orientation is a process, so let yourself explore what is out there and keep an open mind about yourself.

But it's also important to remember that your sexuality (and your gender identity) does not define who you are. We are all a combination of all the different things that we love doing: dancing, drawing, gaming, playing sports – trading Pokémon cards – sitting watching TV with a pizza! Your sexuality is only *one* part of who you are – there is so much more to all of us. So, try not to stress. Keep doing the things you love, being with the people you like and, eventually, the answers you need will come.

♡ Things change

Attractions are like all feelings – they can change, or grow stronger, or disappear altogether. Respect yourself by listening to what your body and heart are telling you – without making assumptions about yourself. Take time to sit with your feelings before labelling yourself as one thing or the other. Learning about your own body, coming to an understanding of what you like and don't like, is just you being you.

Whoever you are attracted to – same sex, opposite sex, all sexes, everybody or nobody – your sexual orientation is something to be celebrated as a part of who you are. Enjoy the feeling of being attracted to somebody, or having a crush on whoever you like, or having no crushes at all without worrying about what it means. Like with other things in life, you don't need to be sure or decide right now.

And remember, when the time comes, *you* get to choose your label – or not choose one at all!

THE LABEL DEBATE

To label or not to label? There are two sides to every story, but there is no right or wrong. Here's how we see it.

RYAN RECOMMENDS!

As you can gather from my story, I'm not a huge fan of labels! I just believe that they can be *so* confusing when you're trying to figure out your sexuality and who you want to be. You might not want to choose a label at all and simply identify as you. It's okay not to know. Experiment and if you don't like something, that's fine. Maybe you don't want a girlfriend or boyfriend, and that's fine too. Maybe everyone around you is getting crushes and you're just not interested in anyone, or you might decide that you are straight but feel an attraction to a same-gender friend. Or maybe you believe you are gay and develop feelings for someone of the opposite gender. You might find yourself attracted to all genders – or none. Whatever you feel, and whoever you are attracted to, is nobody's business but your own. It's no one else's journey but yours, and don't let anyone put their thoughts in your mind – this is *your* life and *your* path, so don't let anyone else walk on it.

You may find labels really helpful, or you might not want to use them at all. As humans, things are not always straightforward or black and white, and some of us just don't like to be defined in any specific way. If you feel yourself getting anxious, like *I must define myself now*, maybe ask yourself *why* you feel the need to do that. Do you feel pressure to fit in with a certain group? Maybe you feel bad about yourself and think that a label will help make you feel more secure? But if you think, *This label feels like 'me', and it's an important part of my identity*, then go for it. Equally, you can completely ignore them. The point is, it is absolutely your choice. The most important thing is that you are doing what feels right for *you*.

The Matthew Facts!

Once I knew I was 100 per cent gay, it felt really good to name it. I actually *love* my label – I'm a gay man! On the other hand, I totally agree with Ryan and think it would be so great if we could all just be who we are. Imagine if we could just be people, without labels – just being *ourselves*. However, that's not happening in the world for a while, so it can be helpful to adopt a practical mindset. Like Ryan, you might not want a label, but it's still important to know what those labels mean so that you can either choose to use one or not to use one.

Sexuality isn't a choice; it's the way someone feels inside and the thing that feels natural to that person. Labels for sexual orientation are not about putting yourself into a box, as our attractions to other people can grow and develop as we grow physically and emotionally. What labels can do is help us to understand ourselves better and give us the language to help define our feelings and attractions. So – whether you choose to use them or not, let's look at what they actually mean.

> FACT! As of 2018, around 2.2 per cent of the UK population identifies as lesbian, gay or bisexual.
>
> Globally – 1 per cent of adults currently describe themselves as transgender, non-binary, non-conforming, gender-fluid or 'in another way', rather than as male or female. Roughly 220,000 of them live in the UK.

♡ Labels: The fundamentals

What do all these letters and labels actually stand for?

You've probably seen the letters 'LGBT' or 'LGBTQIA+' used to describe sexual orientation and/or gender identity. This abbreviation stands for 'lesbian, gay, bisexual, and transgender' or 'lesbian, gay, bisexual, transgender, queer and/or questioning, intersex, and asexual and/or aromantic'. The + (plus sign) is for those in the community who do not fit into any of the specific orientations or who prefer not to use a label; it also includes Allies – which is anyone, of any sexuality or gender, including straight, cisgender people – who wishes to ally themselves with the LGBTQIA+ community. The + is an important part of the label, because it allows parents, friends and supporters of the diverse community to send a message of support out to the world: 'You are LOVED!'

People sometimes get confused about gender and sexuality, but they are two very distinct things (which is why we have given them different chapters in this book). Gender identity is your personal sense of **who you are in terms of gender**, and sexual orientation is **who you are attracted to**. It is very important to understand that people who identify as transgender can be bisexual, queer or straight, depending on how they personally identify.

♡ LGBTQIA+: The basics

Let's explore the diversity of sexual and romantic orientation.

- **Heterosexual [straight]:** Attracted to people of the opposite gender.
- **Homosexual [gay/lesbian]:** Attracted to people of one's own gender.
- **Bisexual:** Attracted to people of more than one gender.
- **Pansexual:** Attracted to people regardless of gender identity. For both bisexual and pansexual people, this can include male, female and non-binary people. (See Chapter Two on gender for a more in-depth look at these labels, including what the acronym 'T' represents!) Different ways people identify to indicate that they are not exclusively attracted to one gender include:

  ▸ Bisexual
  ▸ Pansexual

- (Sexually) Fluid
- Heteroflexible
- Homoflexible
- Queer/Questioning.

• **Aromantic and/or Asexual (ace, aro, aroace** and **acearo):** A person who feels little or no romantic and/or sexual attraction. Some asexual people may still feel sexual from time to time, while others may feel a complete lack of sexual attraction. Some people may feel sexual attraction but no romantic attraction towards others, and some people may feel romantic attraction without feeling sexual attraction. If you feel neither sexual or romantic attraction, you might identify as an **aromantic asexual**.
• The opposite of asexual is **Allosexual:** people who *do* feel sexual attraction; they are not on the ace spectrum.

You can check out the Oxford University LGBTQ+ Society for more on the spectrum of definitions that encapsulate the varying degree and experiences of ace and aro identities.

Remember that sexual orientations and romantic orientations are two different things.

Who you're sexually attracted to (and to what degree) may not reflect who (if anyone) you might be interested to pursue a romantic relationship with. For example, you can feel sexual attraction towards people of the same or different genders but only be romantically attracted to people of the same gender. That's absolutely fine, and you are free to identify however you want regardless of what your attraction to others may look like.

♡ Exploring different things

Finding out what we like is often a process of exploration. Some people just *know* what their preferences are, but most of us, whether it's food or clothes or music, need to take time to try different things before we decide what is right for us.

RYAN

> *'I've had more girlfriends than boyfriends!'*

I feel like I've had more girlfriends than I've had boyfriends, which is so funny to say! I think that me having girlfriends came from a pressure to hide my sexuality and to try to stop people in school from bullying me. I thought that having a girlfriend would make me fit in with the rest of my year and make me feel accepted. But being in a straight relationship was very, very awkward for me because ultimately I couldn't pretend to be something I wasn't. And ultimately, I realised that what I loved about being around my girlfriends was the friendship. After I first kissed my very last girlfriend, we broke up. I basically admitted that I didn't have feelings for her, and I got very emotional. It turned out neither of us actually found the other attractive, but we both loved each other's company. We had both confused having a crush on someone with being friends. We had a very good heart-to-heart, and this actually allowed us to be better friends because once I had let my guard down I was able to be my 100 per cent authentic self. This experience encouraged me to believe that I would eventually grow my confidence, come out, find a guy and be happy.

♡ Give it some time

Growing into yourself, deciding who and what you want to be in life takes time – and your sexuality is no exception. You might be seeing your friends getting girlfriends or boyfriends and saying 'I love you' to each other, which leaves you thinking, *Should I be doing this?* or *I don't know how I feel*. That's OKAY! It really is! You do not have to rush your feelings at all.

Keep an open mind, live in the moment and focus on the people you like at the time that you like them. You don't have to make a decision about who you are now. In fact, you don't *ever* have to decide. Making big decisions about your future life is stressful, and sometimes it's not even necessary. You may learn your taste through trying different things and figuring out what you like, but that doesn't mean that you'll feel the same in the future. It's like asking yourself what you'd like for dinner in three months' time: how could you possibly know now what you want then? It really doesn't have to be a big deal, and it is *so* important that you never feel ashamed of your feelings.

Relationships can be complicated. You might experience sexual feelings for a friend of the same gender or maybe you have a friend who is sexually attracted to you but you might just want to stay friends with them, and this can be confusing too. But how you feel is never, *ever* wrong. Your feelings are your feelings, and again just to repeat, however confusing they can be at times, they are never anything to feel ashamed of.

Finding somebody to talk to along the way can help. You might have a friend or a member of the family who you feel comfortable teasing things out with. If not, there are so many online forums and helplines you can join where people are having these kinds of discussions all the time. Knowing you are not alone will help more than almost anything else.

So, for now, try not to stress. Concentrate on just *being* you without trying to solve questions *about* you. Everyone is different. It honestly takes time to figure out what you want, in all areas of life including, sometimes, our sexual orientation. With time, it will start making sense to you, and you will figure out what feels best whether that comes with a label or not.

♡ The world is changing

Queer people have a much higher profile than they used to have, especially online and in the media. LGBTQIA+ people in the public eye who share their authentic selves with the world can really blaze a trail for those of us who are wondering how our 'differences' might influence the lives we lead.

MATTHEW

> *'The only gay people I saw were on TV.'*

I was exposed to very few gay people growing up. But one evening I was on my bunk bed, flicking through the TV channels when I saw *Will & Grace*. I had never really seen the show before and was instantly hooked when two of the characters were clearly gay; they were very flamboyant like me, and I instantly felt drawn to them. They were just so confident and led such fun lives with their other gay friends. I always felt a kind of excitement watching this show because it gave me hope that if my feelings were true and I did grow up to be gay, I could have a life like theirs, which seemed happy. I then had to deal with my feelings after seeing the show. I felt a range of emotions, including butterflies, knowing I wasn't alone and that being gay was an actual real thing! After being at school surrounded by people getting into 'straight relationships', it opened my eyes and made me realise that there were other people like me in the world.

* * *

Celebrities are more open about their gender and sexuality than ever before:

> *Lil Nas X (rapper, singer)*
> [As a gay rapper] I have even more of a purpose: to continue to find myself and, by doing so, help others find themselves.

> *Kristen Stewart (actress)*
> You're not confused if you're bisexual. It's not confusing at all. For me, it's quite the opposite... The whole issue of sexuality is so grey. I'm just trying to acknowledge that fluidity, that greyness, which has always existed.

> *Miley Cyrus (singer)*
> I don't relate to being boy or girl, and I don't have to have my partner relate to boy or girl. A big part of my pride and my identity is being a queer person.

> *JoJo Siwa (dancer, YouTuber)*
> Technically, I would say that I am pansexual because that's how I have always been. My whole life is just like, my human is my human.

> *Willow Smith (actress)*
> I'm open to polyamory, but I'm not the kind of person that is constantly looking for new sexual experiences. I focus a lot on the emotional connection, and I feel like if I were to find two people of the different genders that I really connected with and we had a romantic and sexual connection, I don't feel like I would feel the need to try to go find more… personally, male and female – that's all I need.

> *Sam Smith (singer)*
> I've always been very free in terms of thinking about sexuality, so I've just tried to change that into my thoughts on gender as well. Non-binary/genderqueer' is that you do not identify in a gender. You are a mixture of all different things. You are your own special creation.

> *Lady Gaga (actress/singer)*
> You know what? It's not a lie that I am bisexual and I like women... This is who I am and who I have always been.

> *Cara Delevingne (model, actress)*
> I always will remain, I think, pansexual... However one defines themselves, whether it's 'they' or 'he' or 'she', I fall in love with the person – and that's that. I'm attracted to the person.

Okay, this is how I feel – what actually am I?

Sometimes we just want to know, and that's perfectly normal. Nobody likes uncertainty so it can be tempting to grab at something before you are really sure. That's okay if it's an online fashion bargain, but it's not a good idea to try to 'identify' yourself too quickly or put yourself in a box just to be classed as something, even though it might seem easier or more straightforward. In that case, perhaps 'queer' or 'questioning' is a great cover-all-bases label if you just want to make it clear that you are 'not straight' and are figuring out how you feel.

The other thing to keep in mind is that you might just *know* – but that doesn't mean you have to *identify* as being straight, gay, bisexual, pansexual, asexual and so on. Remember: you don't have to answer to anyone. You can just *be* you. After all, it's not *what* you are but *who* you are that really counts.

True Life Story: My Two Journeys – Gender Identity and Sexuality

London-based musician and performer Søren (@supersupersoren) tells us their story.

There have been two formative journeys for me – a queer journey and a non-binary journey. From a young age I dealt with the idea that I might be a little different. We all have a favourite Disney film, and for me that was *The Little Mermaid*. I was obsessed with Ariel. It was only later that I found out I wasn't attracted to Ariel, instead I wanted to be her! It isn't black and white. Your brain is going to take you on loads of different journeys, and life will place you in so many different scenarios. It's very likely that you'll feel confused at one point or another. One of the turning points for me was understanding that I didn't relate to what I thought I was supposed to be – a cis gay man.

We're complex human beings. There are many social groups in our community and until I became aware of non-binary gender, I didn't relate to any of them. I couldn't be wrong by default. That understanding came from having trans friends further along their gender journeys than I was. I grew up in the countryside and felt isolated for a very long time. I didn't come out until I moved to London shortly after I turned 19. We shouldn't romanticise these big cities though. There may be a bigger sense of community in the city, but there's no reason you shouldn't make yourself feel seen and heard in the countryside. Politically and socially presenting as a non-binary person is a statement; my family often fear for my safety. You do have to be safe, but equally you can't give up on your identity. Call your mum or a friend if you're traveling home late or if you ever feel unsafe. Whilst it takes a lot of confidence stepping out of the door some days, fashion has always been a safe space for me to express the fluidity in gender and make me truly happy. Bimini from *RuPaul's Drag Race* once said something like – the human existence is so complex that it seems inadequate to tie ourselves down to such strict 'man-made' binaries. I believe that.

Pronouns are always subject to change

While my pronouns have firmed up the last few years, they're always subject to change. We have a broader landscape to exist in. That's the beauty in being non-binary. My current pronouns are they/them – this is what feels the most natural in my life right now. Initially when I started to identify as non-binary, I was using he/they. As time went on, the skews of he/they were shifting towards 'they/them' as that felt more comfortable, embracing both my masculinity and femininity in duality. Dating as a non-binary person can be confusing, but there's no need. We're not defined by who we date, and people shouldn't judge us based on our pronouns alone – we're much more complex than our language. Language can be a tool for freedom, but it can trip you up. We're starting an expression of freedom with 'non' (non-binary); it's kind of ironic! Language can be challenging, but it has to set us free more than it boxes us in.

What do I do about the haters?

Queer folk often like to self-reflect and analyse everything, but we don't have to actively internalise it all. It can have a huge impact on our self-esteem and confidence. I'd advise any young queer person to be more curated with their approach to social media. You should follow LGBTQIA+ influencers, activists and reporters. It'll help you be more aware of the issues that are super important to you and your community. Say it to yourself – I don't need to internalise all of that negative energy. I am not the problem! Find a solid sense of self. I say find because it's hard to just 'have' that; you have to go and look for it. Your identity is not the problem, and that realisation will help set you free. Once you've developed that solid sense of self, go out there and connect with people who share your experiences, find solace in those relationships and let them validate your existence.

Self-love

That being said it can be very difficult online; it can feel like survival. All that negativity all the time can have a significant impact on our mental health and wellbeing. Find those moments of self-love in your day. Look after your body, and safeguard your mental health. Whatever activities make you happy – sports, music, fashion – engage in them. They'll feed your soul. We're so much more than our gender identity and sexuality. Have that moment of separation from the headlines and the internet; we have to enjoy our lives – be happy and be present. Look for those figureheads in music, culture and fashion that make you feel seen. Choose what you're consuming wisely. Put your time and energy into things you believe in – that's what helped me figure everything out and find queer joy.

♡ You are you – we are all different

Embrace the idea that your path is going to be unique.

If you're going through the stage of thinking you might be a lesbian/queer, or other people are telling you that you *are a lesbian/queer* and you're just so confused, don't feel pressured to follow social norms and get a girlfriend or boyfriend for the sake of it.

Obviously if you want to experiment or try different things that's good, but you shouldn't think that you need a boyfriend or girlfriend so people will stop saying that you're gay. Just try to embrace who you are and try not to feel pressured to change the way you live just because of what other people think or say.

You might look at people like us and think, *Oh you know exactly who you are*, but we've been on this journey for ten years. If you are feeling lost and confused, you are not alone. All of us felt like that when we started our journey. We all had days of doubt, worry and anxiety. You might look at us and see a happy, confident LGBTQIA+ couple who have 'made it', but the truth is, we still have days when we doubt ourselves. Growing up is something that never stops, and we continue to question ourselves and grow as people.

It takes time. Your journey is so different from everyone else's so don't compare yourself to anyone else, even us. Sometimes, when we see friends coupling up or classmates who look so confident and sure of themselves, it's easy to imagine that everyone has worked all this stuff out except us. Not to mention all those celebrities whose lives seem *so* perfect! When we are trying to figure out who we are and what we want it's natural to look around and see what other people are doing. But, when we do, sometimes we can feel that life is a competition! The truth is, nobody knows what is really going on inside anybody's head or heart. We are all on our own path, and it's important to enjoy the journey. There's no quick way to finding out who we are. All we can do is listen to our hearts and follow our feelings, and the answers will come. For some people that will be quickly and for others, more slowly.

So, even if you don't feel sure of yourself today, please believe us that the answers will come one day, when you are ready. In the meantime, embrace and enjoy being on your OWN beautiful journey of discovery.

And we're going to help with all the information you need – starting by clearing up some more of LGBTQIA+ common confusions!

♡ Common confusions

Bisexual and pansexual myths that need some serious busting!

We find it really upsetting and annoying when friends come out as bisexual or pansexual and others assume it's a transitioning phase to them coming out as 'fully' gay. It really is a very common confusion, even among people in our community – so, time for some myth busting!

Bi/pan people are just 'confused'.

Figuring out your sexuality can be confusing for everyone, no matter how they identify, but bi/pan people are often accused of being confused – as though they just haven't figured who they're *really* attracted to. That is absolutely not true. Being attracted to more than one or all genders is totally normal – it just means that you can find lots of people attractive!

It's a stepping stone to being gay.

Being bisexual or pansexual isn't a stepping stone to being gay. They are both valid and entirely whole as sexualities.

If you're with a partner of one gender you're not bisexual/pansexual any more.

If you're a boy and you're dating a girl, you can 100 per cent still be bisexual or pansexual. It doesn't become less valid because of the relationship you're currently in. The assumption that you're straight if you're with someone of the opposite gender is completely untrue. You can be in a monogamous relationship with someone of one gender, but that doesn't mean you're no longer attracted to people of other genders.

Bi/pan people are more likely to cheat because they have more choice.

This is such a common misconception and shows a terrible lack of understanding of bisexuality. People don't cheat because they have too much choice. This is an insulting viewpoint that doesn't make sense – on any level.

One day you will have to choose.

There's a myth that younger bisexual/pansexual people are just experimenting and will eventually 'grow out of' their sexuality and become straight or wholly gay. NOT TRUE! Some people change how they identify throughout their lives, and others not at all. Older people can be married to one gender for decades, get divorced, then fall in love with someone of a different gender in old age. Or they stay with people of the same gender. Bisexuality or pansexuality is not a choice.

If you've only ever been with people of one gender, you can't be bi/pan!

It doesn't matter if you've only been with people of different genders to you, you can still identify as bisexual or pansexual. Sexuality comes down to attraction, not experience.

What is bi/pan-erasure?

Most of the above points are to do with a thing called bi/pan-erasure. This is when other people either ignore or re-explain bisexuality and pansexuality. Some people refuse to believe that these sexualities are real, despite the lived experiences of millions. Other people re-label bisexuality and pansexuality as 'gay' or 'straight' depending on who you are dating at that moment. This happens sometimes when celebrities come out as bisexual/pansexual, then appear in public with a same-gender partner and are labelled as 'gay'. And if it's an opposite sex partner, they are sometimes labelled as having gone 'straight'. These attitudes can make bisexual and pansexual people feel as if they don't quite belong within the queer community. Especially if they're dating someone of another gender, they sometimes can feel 'too straight' to, say, attend Pride parades, go to a gay or lesbian bar or participate in community events. Bi/pan-erasure is also a form of…

Bi-phobia!

Narrow-minded opinions about bisexual/pansexual people can often come from straight people as well as other LGBTQIA+ people. There are also people who just don't believe bisexuality/pansexuality exists at all, and often bi and pansexual people are mistakenly labelled as being 'uncertain' or there is the offensive idea that they are greedy and simply want 'everything'. Aside from the trauma and hurt of having your identity erased, bi-phobia can lead to bisexual/pansexual people living in a no-man's land of identity: floating between communities, branded 'too gay' for straight spaces or 'too straight' for LGBTQIA+ spaces. The deepest hurt, though, comes from not being accepted within elements of the LGBTQIA+ community when non-bisexual members say that because bisexuals can benefit from what they call 'straight privilege' they are therefore less entitled to claim pride in their queer identities.

This is so unfair and not true. Bisexual and pansexual people are an integral part of the LGBTQIA+ community and should not have to adjust and amend their own identity to suit other people's perceptions of them.

♡ Okay so, how do I know?

Rainbow Community – tell us how it was for them

Confused? Trust us – it's a work in progress for everyone. Discovering yourself in terms of your sexuality and gender is a given for some and a lifetime journey for others.

We asked our community to send us a few real-life examples of their relationship experiences, in terms of their sexualities.

Anne, 30, heterosexual
I loved my girlfriends but always crushed on boys from a young age but then, when I heard the facts of life, I was horrified! Boys' bodies seemed so unfamiliar. I was also confused because, as I began to develop sexually, I found images of women's bodies way more appealing, so for a while I thought that meant I might be a lesbian. However, in real life, the urge to kiss a woman did not appeal to me, but kissing boys did. At the end of the day I got used to the idea of men's bodies – I think it was just when I was younger that they were strange and unfamiliar to me. My sexuality doesn't feel like a choice.

Katie, 28, bisexual
My boyfriend and I are both bi but we're in a 'straight passing' relationship. Some people find this confusing, because you can't tell from the outside that neither of us is straight! Some people even think that this somehow doesn't count, and because we're in a serious relationship with someone of the opposite gender we're no longer bi. In the past, I've struggled with feelings of not being 'queer enough' and not fitting into the LGBTQIA+ community, but I now know that's not true. We both know who we are and what we're attracted to, and we love each other to bits!

Dave, 26, homosexual
I always liked boys, but when I was about nine I began to pull back from my male friends in school, and I think that was the beginning of realising that I was gay. My feelings for boys were more intense than just boy friendship. My sexual feelings are only towards boys and my romantic feelings too. I have a lot of female friends but when it comes to romance and love? It is boys all the way!

Lauren, 19, bisexual
My first relationship was when I was 14 and I kissed my best friend. We did love each other and had been very close, as friends, since puberty – but on some level we both knew there was more to it. We broke up because I met a guy at a disco and kissed him, and she was really angry. I totally get it and I am not proud of what I did, but now I chalk it up to being a part of discovering who I am. I am sexually attracted

to people from all sexes – and romantically too. You can't choose who you fall in love with.

Kelly, 20, trans lesbian
Being autistic, I've always known I was different. But it took much longer to find out I was also a trans woman. I never really connected with my peers, especially boys, as much as I tried, and have always felt behind them in most ways. By the end of secondary school, I had no real friends there. I never went to any of the discos, never really went out at all. I'd planned to go to the grad ball before it got cancelled, but really I'm glad that didn't pan out.

In retrospect it's easier to see why I avoided all that – knowing whether I had the words or not that it would make me dysphoric, that I would have to act and act and act. At the same time, I could never bring myself to really act. It was a shallow ruse, and I barely had myself fooled. Really, I think I got on better with girls; I just tried so much harder to get on with boys as if to prove something.

The first time I really thought about whether I could be trans was when I realised I was. Before that there were definitely signs, but there was a mental block preventing me from acknowledging it. I feel as if I realised at the time I was most ready to accept it. I'd been taking more of an interest in politics by this point, and left-wing spaces gave me greater perspective on trans issues – I could start to believe it was okay to be trans. Like any other trans person, I still had internalised transphobia to work through. When I realised I was trans I was filled with a lot of dread. Some of it must have been internalised transphobia, but mostly it was knowing things were going to get difficult, that I had to do something about this. But that night before I went to sleep I started to feel hope. I thought to myself, *I'm a girl and that's okay*. I would go back and forth afterwards, but that remains an important moment where I started to accept myself.

Finn, 29, pansexual
For me, the person comes first. I just fall in love, or am really attracted to someone, and I honestly don't care whether they are a man, or a woman, transgender, gender neutral – the attraction is either there or it isn't. I feel fortunate that I can be attracted to anyone regardless of their gender identity. I feel blessed to be this way and to be so open to so many different experiences and people.

Lily, 25, aroace
While all my friends were crushing out at school, I had no idea what they were talking about, but I went along with it. Once, I pretended to have a crush on someone just to fit in, but there was never any feeling there. Right the way through school, nothing, and then in college I found myself standing in the school canteen looking around thinking, *WHY are none of these people ATTRACTIVE?!* Until finally it hit me – it's not them, it's me. I have crazy intense friendships with people (boys, and girls) usually based around mutual interests (gaming, cats) and while I can say I love my friends, it's never romantic. I've had sex a couple of times with a guy who I consider a good friend, so I am not a virgin. It was okay – not unpleasant – because he was a good friend and really enjoyed it, but I'm not in a rush to do it again. I

am quite happy on my own, but my friendships are really important to me (and my cat!).

Kerry, 21, sexually fluid
Honestly? I don't know what I am! I had boyfriends in school, then girlfriends in college. I had a trans lover recently. I guess you could say I am 'pansexual', but I don't like that as a label. I am keeping my options open. When I am in a relationship I am quite conventional. I like being the 'butch' one in a lesbian relationship, but when I am with men I enjoy fitting the more feminine role. I am experimenting in my twenties, but I hope to settle down one day, have a family, children and a dog. But, for the moment? I am having fun being me!

♡ The last word on difference

'You might not be ready to label your feelings and that's okay. It's okay to not know.'
Matthew and Ryan

LOVE IS LOVE MOMENTS
There are so many special moments and memories from our friends and family. Whatever is going on in our lives it's so important to remember that there is always laughter and joy to be found if we look, or even ask for it. When you feel alone, it's important to remember the ways you're connected to the people that love you. We asked our family and friends for joyful moments and fond memories and, of course, embarrassing stories. Maybe you have a few of your own as well?

LOVE IS LOVE MOMENT:
The dye job

When I lived in Southampton, Matthew came round to mine and we attempted to dye his hair blonde.
Let's say the first round of bleach didn't quite go to plan, and we were left with a very yellow head of hair – it was giving Draco Malfoy!

Samara, friend

LOVE IS LOVE MOMENT:
Laugh til it hurts

The boys took me out for a birthday breakfast. I got so many lovely gifts and had a great time. Went to get up, fell straight on my ass and the three of us laughed until it physically hurt (there were tears!).
Ryan never lets me live it down!

Lauren Bagshaw, best friend

LOVE IS LOVE MOMENT:
Friends for life

Me and Matt have had so many great moments together, he's a friend for life. Even though we love each other dearly, we have more of a funny than sentimental friendship – but I trust him with my life! We've had great times together, going to Amsterdam for my birthday and *many* nights out, coaching each other through our twenties and having so many laughs along the way!

Stevie Torbica, Matthew's pal

CHAPTER 2
What's a Pronoun?
And All Things Gender

Gender used to be a *really* clear-cut thing. Back in our parents' day boys wore blue, played with trucks and tractors and were into football. Girls wore pink, played with dolls and were into make-up and fashion. You were either male or female, and everyone was heterosexual.

Some older people claim 'there were no gay people back in my day' and believe gender differences are a fad invented by today's young people.

They could not be more wrong.

The fact is, there have *always* been LGBTQIA+ people in society. The numbers haven't increased; we have just become more visible because society has become more accepting.

> FUN FACT: One hundred years ago people were punished and stigmatised for being left-handed because it was not accepted as 'the norm'. When they stopped punishing schoolchildren for using the 'wrong' hand – figures for left-handed people suddenly soared.

Like left-handedness, the male/female heteronormative perception of society was not how things actually WERE but how they were MADE to be.

However, while attitudes towards non-heterosexuality have improved massively, open conversations around gender identity are still a pretty new thing, and there is still a lot of confusion and controversy around it. The right to identify with and choose your own gender, over the one assigned to you at birth, is one that society is still adjusting to. A lot of people see gender exploration as something 'fashionable' and not a legitimate, personal right to choose one's own identity. There is so much misunderstanding around transgender people too – even in the queer community.

♡ Why did this happen?

It's complicated, but we'll try and unpack it. For centuries, there was black and white thinking that just men and women existed. Men were in charge and women were without power. A male-dominated society like this is called a 'patriarchy'. Within this patriarchy, women had to fight tooth and nail to get basic human rights such as the right to vote (1920 in the USA, 1922 in Ireland, 1928 in the UK). Feminists are people who stand for equal gender rights for women (and this can include men, like us), and for over a century they have fought their cause through political action, protesting and community organisation. At the heart of this was the idea that there are two sexes, male and female, and that they should be equal. (By the way, they are not yet equal – and there is still a long road ahead in this fight.) This inflexible outlook on life is called the gender binary.

Gender binary
So, the gender binary is a viewpoint that divides gender into two distinct and opposing groups: men and women. Because this is a viewpoint that has been around for like, ages, it is taken as scientific fact, but as we have seen above, it is actually the opposite of that. It is an opinion that has BECOME a 'fact' because it simplifies our world, and it makes life easier for a specific type of people (aka straight, white men). The gender binary (which makes us view people as girls or boys, with nothing in between) has created a thing called...

Gender roles
Gender roles are, basically, the expectations that are held by society and people about the actions, thoughts and traits associated with an assigned sex. For instance, gender is influenced by ideas about how men and women should behave, dress and communicate. Western society once believed that women shouldn't be allowed to wear trousers – and some people still believe that men shouldn't wear skirts or dresses. Funnily enough, the colour pink, which we now associate with femininity, was originally only assigned to boys! Society has gendered most things, from clothes to colours, school subjects to sports.

This is thankfully changing each day as our society evolves with more understanding and knowledge. The historically conservative gender binary is really beginning to break down, and there is no going back. It's not just men and women any more. The lines have not only blurred – we are beginning to erase them.

Gender identity
Gender identity is your internal sense of your own gender, your sense of self – it is basically how you feel inside: man, woman, both or neither. Research shows that these feelings about your gender identity can begin as early as the age of two or three and that they can evolve and change over time.

The majority of people feel that they're either male or female. Some people (like us!) feel like a feminine man or, for example, a masculine woman. Some people feel as if they're neither male nor female.

♡ What happens now?

Thankfully, the right to gender self-identification and choosing your own gender is gradually being embraced, not just by the younger LGBTQIA+ community but the older generation and their straight allies. Many young people now declare their correct pronouns, with many allies also asserting theirs in solidarity with the belief that modern, Western male/female ideas of genders are outdated. More than ever before, the LGBTQIA+ community has got behind this and is fighting for transgender rights, and we are now in an era where people of all genders and orientations are increasingly recognised as valid and whole members of society. Gender rights are here to stay, and we embrace and support the trans members of our community.

While we both identify as cisgender males, we understand how gender stereotyping can be really toxic and cause shame and confusion. This was something both of us experienced when we were growing up.

MATTHEW

'Peer pressure was awful.'

I always naturally gravitated to my mum and sister, and women in general, as I just felt more comfortable. I always loved feminine things such as performing Spice Girls' and Britney Spears' songs with my friends, and playing with dolls and Polly Pockets, instead of stuff like Star Wars, WWE wrestling and all the other things other boys at school seemed to like. But there was always something nagging at the back of my mind. One Christmas I was given an Action Man toy and I knew I should have been really excited, but I felt disappointed because I would have rather had a doll like my sister had. It set a seed of doubt that I wasn't doing the right thing. Because of this, for a while I wondered if I wanted to be a girl or if I should have been born a girl because I liked all the things my sister and her friends liked. I grew up confused by society's 'girls like this and boys like that' mentality.

Things got much worse when I became a teenager. Peer pressure took that insecurity to another level. As I grew up, I became more aware that my interests weren't the same as other boys, and I became really uncomfortable within myself. There was such peer pressure to conform to what a boy should be like. I even went through stages of trying to play basketball and attending Scouts in the hope that I could pass as being a 'normal' boy. Everyone was having so much fun at these classes because they really wanted to be there, but I was only there because I wanted to fit in. The sad thing is that if I had wanted to do ballet or 'girly' sports, my parents would have taken me with no problems. But there was always this feeling of 'what will other people think?' I felt I should be doing 'boy' things – even though I didn't enjoy them. There was nobody in my life telling me to do boy things, but I felt it was expected of me, by society I suppose. Why can't we just be who we are without being put in a box?

RYAN

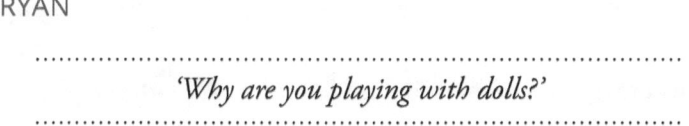

'Why are you playing with dolls?'

At home, I always felt safe to be myself because I mainly spent time with my dad. Dad always got me whatever I wanted to play with, and it was never a problem. I remember one time he bought me this pair of pink plastic heels I wanted when all the other boys were playing football! It was just when I'd go to my friend's house I became aware that I liked different things. I remember playing with dolls in my friend's room, and her brother walked in. And he was just like, 'Why are you playing with dolls? You're a boy!' I remember thinking, maybe I should keep this a secret. The next time I went to my friend's house I had to ask if her brother was at home because I didn't want that awkward conversation again. That incident definitely changed my outlook on me playing with dolls – and later on, make-up – and I started getting a little bit more secretive.

Being a boy who liked wearing make-up as a teenager was not easy. I was teased for wearing the most subtle of lip-gloss! Make-up made me feel good about myself, but other people's spiteful comments made me feel bad about it. I suppose I have always been quite feminine, and it wouldn't take a genius to realise I was gay. As teenagers, people notice things more and point things out to you. Even when they weren't being horrible, it still put a magnifying glass over my feelings, so I started to think about it more and become conscious of my femininity. It made me feel more awkward in certain situations. I worried about how I should act, if I should change myself to fit in. It was small things – I remember thinking about not bringing anything pink to school in case I got bullied for it. I let go of things that I really enjoyed, and I think that's sad.

I never felt that wearing make-up was a masculine or feminine thing for me; it's just always been something I love to do. Making up my face is my form of creative expression. I feel more like myself when I have my face on. It's always been important for me to always be accepted as myself. Not 'boy' or 'girl' – just 'Ryan'.

♡ Why gender is important

We all deserve to be our authentic selves, to live our lives fully being who we want to be, and feeling happy with our gender is an important part of that. Some people transition fully to another gender than the one they were assigned at birth, and others are fluid: they feel like being a boy some days, and a girl other days, or like neither. Many people are gender neutral and just want to be 'themselves'.

As gay men, we both happily identify with as he/him/his pronouns. But gender equality issues in our community have really opened our eyes. We believe there shouldn't be any assumptions about gender. We would love to see a world where nobody had to identify specifically as he or she or they – we would all just be people.

In the meantime, gender equality rights are at the very heart of the LGBTQIA+ community, and it is our job to educate people against transphobia and try to create a world where everyone is accepted.

When the subject comes up in conversation with people of our parents' and grandparents' generation, we have found that it can sometimes be a difficult concept for older people to take in. Their objections are usually based around fear and misunderstanding because the gender spectrum was never an option given to them to explore and seems to have come out of the blue. It is not something everyone has experience of or understands, so if someone is genuinely interested in your point of view, be patient and try to explain it to them.

However, it is also worth noting that some individuals and communities, for a variety of reasons, including strongly held religious beliefs, can have hostile attitudes towards transgender topics and people. If that's the case, it's best to stay safe and walk away.

Nobody should have to explain or defend who they are, and the good news is that transgender people have never been more in the public eye.

Actor Elliot Page publicly came out as transgender in 2020 and became the first trans man to feature on the cover of *Times* magazine.

Actors and activists Chaz Bono and Laverne Cox star in the brilliant documentary *Disclosure*, which has been a game-changer for showing the world what the people in the transgender community have gone through on their journey to be accepted.

Hollywood has begun to write more gender-diverse roles with actors like Elliot Fletcher making a career of portraying young transgender characters like Aaron in *The Fosters*.

American model Hari Nef paved the way for a lot of new trans models when she became one of the first openly transgender people to be signed by powerhouse modelling agency IMG and was followed by the stunning Dutch model Valentijn De Hingh. Australian model Andreja Pejić was the first openly transgender model profiled by *Vogue*.

'There is an extreme lack of representation for young, deaf, queer, Jewish, Asian, transgender artists… So, I decided to be my own representation,' said Chella Man, model, activist and artist.

We love that! Standing up and speaking your truth takes courage, and it's important that the people who do it can feel the support of the rest of our community around them.

♡ Let's get started!

It can be daunting when faced with the vast amount of information that's out there, but our hope is to help you make sense of the basics. Keep in mind that the majority of people don't know everything about *everything* – it's normal! But, taking the time to familiarise yourself with the fundamentals can disprove stereotypes or untruths you might have soaked in from the world without realising.

P/S: By no means should this be your only or main source of information about gender, but we hope it can be a springboard to encourage (and entice!) you to learn about it on a deeper level.

♡ Back to those labels again!

Now, you've seen how we think about labels and that labels aren't for everyone, and they are not something anyone should feel pressured into using. However, it's a fact that, as humans, lots of us find comfort and understanding in labels. They can help us describe our feelings – and the lens we view life through. None of us likes being seen as something that we are not, so it can be important to tell people who you are and how you would like to be referred to. Labels can put things into perspective, and there are so many of them because the human experience is diverse and unique to each person.

♡ Why we love language (and we don't just mean talking!)

Language was created to help us communicate and connect with one another; the more words we learn that describe *all* life experiences, the more we understand – and the more we can empathise.

Language – and labels – can affirm our identity. Whether we call ourselves lesbians or Disney fans, giving ourselves a label can boost our self-confidence, empowering and facilitating us to share our authentic self with others. Labels are meant to describe our experience but not be the only picture – they do NOT define who we are as a person.

In many cases, the labels we give ourselves can enable us to form relationships with people who share our identities and help us assimilate into a wider community or group. The language used within the LGBTQIA+ community is incredibly varied because we are all so different.

Gender and sexual orientation are, of course, two completely different things.

To us, it is obvious that we are both guys, so we find it *really* annoying when people assume that Ryan plays the 'feminine' role in our relationship just because he wears make-up.

However, maybe it is not always as obvious as we think.

Ryan wears make-up. We know that Ryan is a *boy* who likes to wear make-up because it makes him feel good, and it is just a part of who he is as a person. However, *some* 'boys' choose to wear make-up as a conscious part of their transitioning process. Or if they are gender fluid, they might wear make-up when they want to identify as more feminine on that particular day. Some people wear make-up as a statement of gender, and others, like Ryan, just wear it to make themselves feel good.

The bottom line is – as we said at the beginning of this chapter – it doesn't matter. Life would be SO much easier if we all just accepted and enjoyed each other as human beings instead of caring how exactly we each identify. Maybe one day that will happen but – for now – there is a whole world out there that needs educating about all things LGBTQIA+.

And with that, let's get into learning a bit about the gender aspect of our community.

RYAN RECOMMENDS

Science – not my greatest subject in school but hey – this is so IMPORTANT (and, by the way, fascinating!), so I'll break it down for you guys as best I can!

ASSIGNED SEX: MALE, FEMALE, INTERSEX.

As we all know, we each begin our life being born as a baby. When that happens, a doctor labels the baby with an **assigned sex**.

They do this by looking 'downstairs' – if you know what I mean – at the baby's genitals (and chromosomes) and they note down if the baby is a girl (female) or boy (male). This then goes on their birth certificate. Job done – EXCEPT, unbeknownst to most of us there is a third label aside from 'female' and 'male' called 'intersex'. **Intersex** is an umbrella term that refers to individuals whose bodies are naturally different from what is typically classified as female or male.

I AM BEWILDERED. WHY DOES NOBODY KNOW THIS?!

Intersex people have chromosomes, hormones and/or body parts that differ from typical definitions of female/male sexual and reproductive anatomy. Sometimes these intersex traits are identified at birth, while, for others, they are not identified until later in life (or not at all!). Some well-known intersex people include model Hanne Gaby Odiele and filmmaker, actor and model River Gallo.

And here is the newsflash – being intersex is a **natural biological variation** which happens in around 2 per cent of all births.

> FUN FACT: The birth of redheads
> has a similar percentage!

This just goes to show that, despite intersex being a widely unknown term, it's really not that unusual.

Woah! The common retort 'man and woman are the only sexes – it's natural!' is, in fact, false. It is actually natural to have more than two sexes.

So why don't we know this? That is where the **gender binary** comes back in.

It can be easy to confuse the meanings of all of these new words. So, don't be too hard on yourself and let's have a quick recap:

- **Assigned sex** is the gender presumed for you at birth based on your biology, anatomy and chromosomes.
- **Intersex** is a term that describes people who, naturally, don't fit typical male/female presentations.
- **Gender binary** is a classification system that believes there are only two genders: men and women. This forms society's set of expectations, standards and characteristics about how men and women are supposed to act.

- **Gender roles** are societal expectations that dictate how we should act, speak, think, dress, groom and interact with others.

It's a lot. Especially if these terms are new for you. Maybe you recognised some of the concepts I described, even if you didn't know the words for them.

Science bit over.

Now – got that? Good. I'mmma gonna hand you over to Matthew for the rest – I need a lie down!

The Matthew Facts

Thank you to Ryan for setting the stage. Let's get right into the meanings of those 'buzz words' you hear all the time. Carrying on from where Ryan left off, your gender identity is *your* sense of your own gender. If the gender you identify with is the same as the one you were assigned at birth, this is known as cisgender (cis for short). If the gender you identify with is different from the one you were assigned at birth, you may identify as transgender (trans for short), or non-binary.

So, **cisgender** refers to people whose gender identity aligns with their assigned sex. Ryan and I identify as cisgender men.

Transgender is an umbrella term that broadly refers to anyone who doesn't identify with their assigned sex. This includes binary trans people (trans women and trans men) and non-binary people. Some people who cross-dress also identify as trans.

Non-binary is a word that describes people who feel that their gender lies outside the bounds of the gender binary. The term encompasses people who do not fit into the stereotypical ideas of male or female; they may identify with both or neither. Non-binary is also an umbrella term for the varied, inclusive labels that further describe non-binary people's gender. Some examples of these are genderqueer, two-spirit, genderfluid and agender.

It's important to note that not all non-binary people identify as trans.

So, let's have a quick re-cap:

- **Gender identity** is how you feel. Girl. Boy. Both. Neither.
- **Cisgender** is when you identify with the sex you were assigned at birth.
- **Transgender** is when you *don't* identify with the sex you were assigned at birth.
- **Non-binary** is when your gender identity can't be defined by 'woman' or 'man'. There are many different gender-neutral/non-binary identities.

It's important to note that our gender can be *expressed* in a variety of different ways; some universal examples include clothing, behaviour and pronouns. Often – because of the gender binary – people assume someone's gender based on these factors. However, you cannot guess a person's gender or their pronouns by how they outwardly express themselves, nor should you. But, what's the story with pronouns? Let's take a closer look…

Pronouns

Pronouns are short words we all use to describe people instead of using their name: 'he has gone to the shop', 'they left their phone over there', 'she passed her driving test' and so on.

Binary pronouns (pronouns that fit within the categories of 'woman' or 'man') include: she/her/hers and he/him/his. Non-binary people may also choose these pronouns, or they may feel more comfortable with the use of gender-neutral pronouns (pronouns that do not fit the categories of 'woman' or 'man') such as they/them/theirs. Some non-binary people choose a variety of them.

If you are unsure about someone's pronoun, ask them. Perhaps you'll want to share your pronouns as well.

You may be thinking what is the big deal, or that none of this is even relevant to you. Yet, using people's correct pronouns (which is affirming gendered language) has proven to have a huge, positive impact on trans and non-binary people's mental health as it enables them to feel gender euphoria or a harmony with their gender identity. This can make them feel delight, comfort, relief, joy and excitement. And in that case, it's always best to use people's correct pronouns when possible.

Gender dysphoria

Often, when trans people are reminded of the fact that their gender differs from the one they were assigned at birth, they experience intense distress and discomfort; this is called **gender dysphoria**. This can be triggered by their bodies (physical dysphoria), such as their hair/voice/body shape, or socialisation (social dysphoria). An example of this could be someone misreading their gender and using incorrect pronouns.

Many young (and older) trans people struggle with isolation and depression and this sometimes leads to self-harm and even suicide. The most vital remedy and preventative measure is giving young trans people the support and acceptance that they need. This means making sure trans children know that they are loved, unconditionally, for exactly who they are.

It can be difficult to have compassion for things that we don't understand, or that we understand but only linguistically. We can also be afraid to say the wrong thing or accidentally offend someone.

The only solution here is to see transgender people as *people* – not as their gender identity. Follow trans and non-binary people on social media. Get information from a diverse variety of sources. Understand that trans people are not – and should not be – defined by their transness. Just like any cisgender person, transgender people are multi-faceted human beings. If not for how society treats trans people, the trans experience wouldn't have to be a struggle – it could be a seamless fact. Without transphobia, perhaps transitioning would be akin to 'the gender I was assigned at birth is a mistake so I'm fixing it'. Maybe there's an even more progressive reality where gender roles don't exist at all.

At the end of the day, affirming trans people's gender identity is proven by research to benefit their health and overall satisfaction in life. It costs us little, if anything at all, to make a concentrated effort to put aside our preconceived ideas or prejudices and genuinely listen to and learn from trans educators.

♡ Common confusions

What's the difference between trans and non-binary?

Transgender people may still fit into binary (female/male) identities and identify with binary pronouns, whereas non-binary people do not conform to traditional binary gender – they identify with neither, both or a mixture of the two – and often use gender-neutral pronouns.

Are intersex people non-binary?

At birth, intersex people are commonly assigned a sex. This implies that even while they have a variety of unique requirements that set them apart from cisgender people, they can go unnoticed because of the gender that was ascribed to them at birth. Some intersex people identify as non-binary while others do not; it can depend on each individual's experience and whether they feel safe and included in non-binary spaces. The word intersex is NOT synonymous with the term non-binary.

What are dead names?

A dead name is the name that was given to a transgender person at birth. This name is no longer used if they change their name as part of their gender transition.

Do you have to experience gender dysphoria to be trans?

The short answer: no. The longer answer: gender dysphoria can often be an indicator for people that they're trans, but it is not a requirement for someone to identify as or be trans.

What is the difference between transsexual and transgender?

Transsexual is a medical term that has been used historically to describe individuals who have undergone some type of medical and/or surgical treatment for their gender affirmation. Transgender is a non-medical term that refers to non-cisgender people, as Matthew discussed above. Transgender is the preferred term, unless specified otherwise.

What is transphobia?

Transphobia is when someone is prejudiced against transgender and gender non-conforming people. Acting on this is a hate crime.

♡ What's your pronoun?

People's pronoun usage across their ages, sexuality and gender is not always what you would expect – and it's made us think about 'labels' in a new way too. Instead of being shoved into boxes, pronouns can give us a chance to identify ourselves in a way that is more thought provoking.

We hope these pronoun stories might inspire you to explore the reasons behind your own choice of pronouns if you haven't done so already.

Susan, 27, supermarket manager, cis woman, heterosexual
Pronouns: them/they/theirs, she/her/hers

I am a straight cis woman who identifies in everyday life as a she/her but in social media and public life as they/them. They/them pronouns honour my life experience that I am a gender-neutral human being before I am a 'woman'.

Tammy, 21, writer/retail worker, gender fluid, pansexual
Pronouns: she/her/hers, he/him/his, they/them/theirs

I use all pronouns because the way I feel towards being male, being female, being a mixture of both or neither changes as often as the phases of the moon. As such, so do my pronouns, but most often I find that they/them gives me a happy little kick every time. It makes me feel, even on the boy days and even on the girl days, like I'm still being seen – not as one or the other – but as a being capable of change, like I'm being seen as me.

Eoin, 20, student/cleaner, gay, cis man
Pronouns: he/him/his

I chose these pronouns as I believe they are what best describes me and the gender I identify as. They are also what makes me feel most comfortable therefore I have never considered any other pronouns.

Pearl, 21, student writer, queer, cis woman
Pronouns: she/her/hers

I go with these pronouns because they seem to fit me best. I've always identified with my womanhood, or what I perceive to be womanhood: my sensuality, my compassion, my social awareness. I don't think those traits are inherently female but, for me, they're interwoven in my identity as a woman – and, I suppose, she/her pronouns best encapsulate that for others.

Gwen, 19, student, non-binary, bisexual
Pronouns: she/her/hers, he/him/his, they/them/theirs

When it comes to my gender, I'm quite apathetic. I present quite feminine, but I don't necessarily feel female. I envy the way cis boys can be feminine or the way some people's gender is so ambiguous. I've grown up being called a girl/daughter and other female terms, so I'm used to being classified as a woman, but even though I don't resent being called a girl or likewise, I still know I'm more comfortable not aligning myself with gender norms. I still and will continue to experience misogyny, but that doesn't come down to how I present; misogyny derives from the gender norms and standards. Being assigned 'woman' or 'man' from birth already paints a child's life out. So that's why I feel most comfortable identifying as non-binary.

Orien, 21, *student, cis woman, queer*
Pronouns: she/her/hers, they/them/theirs
I have never felt completely comfortable sitting within the bounds of 'woman'. There are many facets of my identity that don't feel as if I can be fully connected to womanhood.

Kris, 21, drag queen, cis male, gay
Pronouns: he/him/his, they/them/theirs
While I wholly 'live' my female identity as a drag performer, I identify as male in everyday life. However, I do not adhere to gendered rules of dress and would prefer if nobody was gendered, and for that reason I use the pronouns they/them.

Ronnie, 20, student, transgender, gay
Pronouns: he/him/his

Even though I have felt like a boy all my life, dressed in a male way, I did not feel the need to identify as specifically male until I began a relationship with my boyfriend. I changed my name and have begun to identify publicly as male in the last six months. Committing to my male pronoun is my first step in a full transitioning process.

Kit, 23, student journalist, transgender, lesbian
Pronouns: she/her

My parents still see me as their 'son', which is really hard and affects my confidence and how I am able to live my female identity. I have begun my transition, which gives me body confidence, but it still makes a huge difference when people use my pronoun. My main tutor in college this year asked everyone to introduce themselves by their chosen pronoun on our first day and even though it felt strange announcing my gender publicly, it also was empowering. Every time somebody uses my pronoun, it feels like a gift. It's so important to me.

Sam, 27, computer programmer, straight, cis man
Pronouns: he/him, they/them

My partner is a transgender woman. To me, she is fully a woman – that is how I see her. Although her transition is not complete in medical terms, I am very happy with her and love the way she is. I want her to be happy and whatever she chooses to do, or not do, to her body, I will always support her. I fit the stereotype of he/him, and Kim is very glamorous – *all* woman! I use the they/them pronouns on all my social media to support the cause of transgender issues. Some of the lads are a bit thick and tease me for being gay or bi, but I don't really care. I'm happy with Kim and they are probably just jealous! 'They' is a pronoun I use because it is my way of saying it doesn't really matter. I'm not hung up on it either way. Just living my best life being who I am with my best girl.

Matthew & Ryan chat with...

Whitney and Megan Bacon-Evans, **both lesbian.** Content creators, businesswomen and LGBTQIA+ activists.
Together they are @whatwegandidnext

M&R: You met while on opposite sides of the world. Can you share with us a bit about how you met and how different your lives were growing up as LGBTQIA+ in your respective countries?

Whitney: We actually met on MySpace! For those who don't know MySpace was THE social networking platform back in the day, prior to Facebook. I actually found Megan through what I call a 'divine intervention' on Christmas eve. I was home in Kentucky from Hawaii for Christmas break and feeling jet lagged. I always had a thing for British accents so decided to search on MySpace for British girls. In order to do this, you had to input a postcode into the browse section. I had to google (or maybe 'yahoo') to find a British postcode. I put it into MySpace, and there was Megan on the first page! I added her as a friend, and luckily she accepted!

Megan: Fast forward a couple of years later and Whitney studied abroad in London for a semester in 2008. We had started communicating a lot, but just as friends even though we both secretly were hoping for it to be more! We met up the first weekend after she landed in the UK and instantly hit it off. We had our first kiss in a lesbian bar in London, Candy Bar, and two weeks later we were officially girlfriend and girlfriend! The rest as they say is history, or herstory!

W: I'm a Southern girl – I was born in Tennessee and raised in a small religious town in Kentucky. It was hard growing up knowing that I'm gay but wishing the feelings away. I struggled for a long time and was even outed by one of my so-called friends when I was 15! This led to my friends turning against me, and also my mom reacted really badly; it was a really tough experience to go through. However, as soon as I started to accept who I am and feel confident in that, no one else cared! I decided I needed to leave Kentucky to become the person I'm meant to be, which is why I moved to Hawaii to study my degree and then ultimately ended up in England with the love of my life!

M: While I grew up in England, I had a similar experience to Whitey with my mum not accepting that I'm gay. I came out aged 16, and it turned out my best friend was also into girls! Everyone was accepting, apart from my mum, and it took her a couple years to come around, but like Whitney's mom, they're both super accepting now and love us both like their own daughters!

M&R: You call yourselves 'long distance love survivors'. Can you tell us a bit about how that worked for you?

W: We ended up doing long distance between Hawaii and the UK for four years, due to a denied visa extending the journey.

M: It was definitely tough to go through but absolutely worth it! This was between 2008 and 2012, so FaceTime didn't even exist! We kept our relationship going mainly through long diary-type entries via Facebook messenger. Due to the time difference being 11 hours, we would leave each other messages about our day for the other to read when they woke up. We'd also send each other videos, and we tried to Skype but technology often failed us!

W: It helped to have a date in mind when we would next visit one another. Somehow we managed to see each other pretty much every three to four months. We kept going as we knew we'd achieve the end goal of being together and that it would all be worth it. Which it was! I've been living in the UK with Megan for over 10 years now!

M&R: Your wedding looked so beautiful – what was the highlight of the day for you?

M&W: Thank you! It really was the best day. Of course getting to marry one another was our highlight but also having all of our friends and family from USA and UK together for the first time was such a highlight and so much fun! Everyone says it's the best wedding they've been to, and of course we agree!

M&R: As two self-named 'Femme/lipstick' lesbians – how do you feel about gender stereotyping?

M: Growing up we didn't have any femme lesbian role models to look up to. I certainly felt like the only femme in the world and wondered if there were others out there like me! The stereotype for lesbians back then definitely was short hair and masculine clothes, which just never was my identity. The lack of visibility is actually one of the reasons that I put our faces online back in 2009, to try to provide representation for anyone else struggling and wondering if a love like they hope for exists.

W: Now there is so much for representation and variety in presentation. As visible femme lesbians, we break the stereotype for what some people may still think a lesbian looks like. Over the years we've been told 'you don't look gay' or 'you're too pretty to be gay'. But no one looks gay or straight; there is no one look. How you express your gender has no correlation to your sexual orientation. We still get assumed to be straight, and more often, sisters… or even mother and daughter despite being one year apart in age!

M&R: Have you any advice to give a young person who might be getting bullied for being 'different'?

W: You don't see this now, but being different is your super power! Count yourself lucky that you are unique… who wants to be normal? How boring life would be!

M: What you go through will make you the person you're meant to be. Stay strong and know that you are SO loved and will live a happy and fulfilled life! Just remember that your bullies are normally going through something in life to make them that way.

M&R: You are role models for a lot of young people. What are the main issues that you think are facing young LGBTQIA+ today?

W: Aw thank you! While we have come so far in so many ways, it's still illegal to be LGBTQ+ in 72 countries. We can't travel as freely as heterosexual couples and always in the back of our mind have to worry about our safety, no matter where we are in the world.

M: We've also been campaigning for fertility equality for same-gender female couples, as we discovered there's discrimination and an unfair financial burden that is being placed on the LGBTQ+ community. While the Government have announced plans to remove barriers for same-gender female couples to receive fertility treatments from April 2023, we have yet to receive further details as to when this will exactly be rolled out. We hope that by the time the younger LGBTQ+ community have children, that they won't have to face the same burdens and discrimination. The cost is even greater for same-gender male couples going through surrogacy, and equality for that looks to be a long way ahead.

M&R: What does Pride mean to you?

M&W: Pride is when everyone comes together, and you know that you're more than just accepted, you're loved. We're proud to be our authentic selves 24/7 and to show others that you can stay true to who you are and be more than happy! We're proud to live our lives as wife and wife and as part of the beautiful LGBTQ+ community!

♡ Last word on gender

'Nobody should be judged for being who they are. Every person is an individual. Every human being is different, and we all have the right to be ourselves.'

True Life Story: 'Betrayal'

Liberty, a 20-year-old trans writer, tells us her conflicted story of gender and sexuality.

Lately I've been struggling with being a trans lesbian.

Whenever I like a girl, I feel a lot of guilt. My fear of rejection is twofold. On the one hand, rejection must make me unlovable. On the other hand, it makes me a bad person. Predatory in some way. That I could like someone without permission. Rationally, this doesn't really make sense. But it's a feeling that consumes me.

As a trans woman, I'm told that I'm invading women's spaces. If I go to the female toilets, I'm making other women around me feel unsafe. According to transphobes, I go through all the effort to appear feminine, taking hormones and all, just so I can be a predator. Although the men's bathroom is objectively more dangerous for trans women, many of us fear the women's bathroom more. It's the fear that someone might be scared of us. The fear that someone will see a monster, an alien. And though we might protest this idea, say it's ridiculous (how does it hurt you?) at the end of the day it's easy to internalise.

I feel similarly about being attracted to women. The idea of a trans lesbian seems to shock people. I get confused looks when I say I'm a lesbian even from otherwise supportive people. Some people, whether they realise it or not, seem to have the idea that attraction to trans women is abnormal. Straight men don't like them, it's a sign he's a little gay! Any trans woman knows that's false, but to cis people a straight man liking us is always some shocking reveal. The same must be thought of cis lesbians – that they could never like someone like me. Every now and then the tabloids write an article about how trans women are forcing cis lesbians to date us lest they be labelled transphobic, and that's ridiculous. First, we trans women don't seek out people disgusted by us. Second, nobody is forced to like us. It's not an act of deception. If you like women, ultimately you will like trans women.

But again, I know all this and still feel that fear when I like a girl. That when I like someone it's somehow predatory. That when someone likes me they have been deceived of my true nature. That I've betrayed a secret code among women. In a way, I have. A lot of women connect to each other by their attraction to men. A lot of trans women can make cis women feel a little more at ease through this. Being a lesbian, this is something I'll never understand. Sometimes I almost wish I would. It wouldn't come with the same baggage, the same guilt.

I know that I'm nothing like the cis straight men who openly objectify women, who reduce us to sex objects, who barely see us as human. But I can't help the feeling that I'm some kind of monster too, that I somehow betray women every time I fall in love with one.

I wish it didn't have to be like this. Society is changing, but, for me, it can't happen quickly enough. I long for a time when I can be who I want and love who I want without feeling guilty, or wrong or weird about it.

When we can all truly be open about ourselves, it will be so much easier to find partners who will love us for who we are. Betrayal happens when we have to lie about ourselves by hiding who we are away.

I am not hiding any more.

LOVE IS LOVE MOMENT:
Look after each other

I was in a rough place earlier this year, and Matthew and Ryan couldn't have been more supportive. They were there for me every step of the way, never judged me and always accepted me. I honestly don't know where I would be without them both and I am SO glad they found each other!

Lauren Bagshaw, best friend

LOVE IS LOVE MOMENT:
Celebrating your joy

A special moment for me is seeing them both grow and develop into the amazing humans I know today! I don't think I will ever get used to them being approached in the middle of the street by fans wherever we go! I am so proud of both of them and how hard they have both worked to achieve their dreams, I couldn't be happier for them both!

Samara, friend

CHAPTER 3

Coming Out

Or Inviting In

Coming out is the first thing that comes up when you think you might be LGBTQIA+. People might be asking you, 'Oh, have you come out yet?' or 'When are you coming out?'

There is so much expectation around it, so much pressure. The very thought of having to sit down and tell someone else something so personal as your gender or orientation can make you feel exposed and vulnerable. And there is a good reason for that.

The phrase 'coming out' dates back to the bad old days where homosexuality was illegal, and gay people lived their lives secretly, hiding themselves away in what was referred to as 'the closet'. When gay men and women took the brave step of declaring they were gay, it was called 'coming out of the closet'.

Thankfully, people who are LGBTQIA+ no longer have to hide as much, so, technically, we should no longer be obliged to 'come out'. So why don't we find new language, and new frameworks, for sharing LGBTQ+ identity? We shouldn't have to 'come out' any more. Instead, we should be 'inviting in' the world, at a time that we choose.

The act of sharing this information about yourself with other people should not be *you coming out* of a dark corner and looking for acceptance. Instead, you *can invite them in* and share something important and meaningful about yourself with them.

♡ All about you

So the first thing to say is, coming out/inviting in is all about you. It is your choice to disclose or not disclose personal information about yourself, when/if ever it feels right and with whoever you feel safe with. Even though we both chose to come out to our family and friends, it is also important to recognise that many people choose to keep their orientation and gender to themselves and don't feel any obligation or desire to share it. And that is absolutely normal. You might be thinking *Why should I come out? Do I need to come out?* Or simply, thinking that it's not that much of a big deal. Everyone is different, and everyone's *journey* is different. The important thing is to not get stressed or worried about whether you do or don't. It's also okay to tell certain people your sexuality but not the rest of the world. Not 'coming out' is not the same thing as *hiding* your sexuality from people because you are ashamed of it. It is simply that you don't want to share that information about yourself, and you should never feel obliged to 'invite in' anyone to your personal space unless you absolutely want to.

Coming out/inviting in is everyone's personal choice. Some people don't feel the need to justify their sexuality to everyone, but, for some people, it is important to clearly let others know who they are. The important thing is to make the choice that will allow you to be your happy and authentic self.

Our personal coming out stories are both quite different…

MATTHEW

'Coming out at school helped me be myself but it wasn't an easy ride.'

I was constantly acting out around friends and other people in the classroom as if I was really moody because I wanted attention. But when anyone asked me, I would say nothing because I was too scared to come out. I was still good friends with my ex-girlfriend, and she could tell that something was wrong and wanted to talk to me, so I agreed to be honest with her. I remember my heart beating like crazy, and I was feeling really anxious yet really excited because I was finally going to tell someone who I really was and what I was feeling inside for all these years. I kept saying that I couldn't tell her. But then she suggested a game; she would ask me three things about what could possibly be wrong with me, and I had to say yes to one of them if it was true. The first thing was that I wanted to run away, the second thing was that I was gay, and the third thing was something silly she'd made up to make me smile. Of course, I gave in, and in a burst I screamed that I was gay. I was instantly worried about her reaction because she had been my girlfriend for a few months, and I worried that she would think she had turned me gay, but I also felt a release of 'Oh my God, I've told someone'.

Her reaction was really positive, and she was like, 'Oh my God, I knew it! This is great!' and it was just a huge feeling of relief that I'd finally told someone, and I hadn't been told that I was disgusting or gross. I thought this would stop the need to tell people who I really was, that telling one person would be enough for a while, but it wasn't.

Telling someone and getting a positive reaction was exhilarating, but then I thought of going straight back into the claustrophobic closet. It was like a switch was flipped inside; I made the decision to just say that I was gay to people who asked, and I allowed her to tell people we trusted. I'm not sure what came over me to start sharing it like this, but I just wondered what I really had to lose in telling people. Did I really want to be friends with, or surround myself with, people who wouldn't like the news anyway? So, I just told them.

It began spreading around the school like wildfire.

Most people were really positive, which gave me a burst of confidence. It was like, yes, people know that I'm gay, and I don't have to hide it. However, there was a group of friends who instantly rejected me for it. It was really strange because I had built this up for so long as if I was going to be an absolute mess if I was rejected, but it really is shocking how strong you can become when you need to be. I was slightly concerned that I was going to get beaten up or bullied the next day at school, but at the same time I didn't really care because I was so happy that people finally knew the real me.

After I came out at school, life was so much easier. I went off and played rounders with the girls, and the boys were all waving – being really nice to me – no problem. Being my authentic self made life so much easier.

Strangely, the next day, the people who had rejected me online the night before quickly apologised to me and began to accept me. Although this left me feeling really confused and conflicted, with lots of emotions pulling at me, I wanted it to be as easy as possible and minimise any potential future clashes. I just accepted the apology and didn't question them on it. I still had some teasing from boys telling me not to fancy them or worried that they would 'catch' being gay, but even then other people would stick up for me. It made life a bit easier in terms of being able to do PE with the girls instead of being forced to do sports like rugby where I felt really uncomfortable with boys. The funny thing is that none of the teachers or support workers ever checked in on me or asked me if I was okay. Looking back now, I was riding such a high from finally feeling able to be myself at school, but it breaks my heart knowing that I had no one to really share the emotional stress of it all with. I kept batting it away because I wanted to focus on the positives of being accepted at school.

> *'I decided not to tell my family that*
> *I was gay and only tell people at school.'*

Telling everybody at school and telling my family felt like two completely different cans of worms because I didn't feel comfortable enough to confide in my family yet. It was one big hurdle doing it at school, but coming home to normality was an escape from it all. It wasn't that I was scared of being rejected by my family, just that it wasn't a conversation I felt comfortable having.

However, I did eventually tell my mum a few years later. I was so nervous in the lead-up as I texted her asking her to come up to my bedroom. My heart was pounding hearing her footsteps coming up the stairs, but I had a strange burst of relief begin to come over me as I told her. Mum told me that she had always known; she wondered how I thought she wouldn't guess because my bedroom as an 18-year-old was covered in Justin Bieber, Britney Spears and Beyoncé posters – I was obviously, clearly gay. The conversation lasted around 30 seconds, and we've never really spoken about it since, it was just instantly accepted. I don't really know what else I expected. Her reaction was accepting but calm, and I felt slightly underwhelmed but also relieved after all the build-up. It quite simply wasn't a big deal at all, and things didn't change at home. I felt so grateful a little later that I didn't have to deal with a huge, negative coming-out family experience.

RYAN

'I had enough of hiding and really wanted to tell someone.'

The first person I came out to was my best friend when we were in Year 10. We both got bullied and picked on, but we were there for each other. We both saw each other cry, we both saw each other laugh, and we just had a really great friendship. She knew everything about me, and it got to the point where I didn't want to hide such a huge part of who I was from my best friend.

At this point, I was feeling really isolated from everyone at home, struggling at school, and I felt as if I had to constantly hide who I was. But it was also getting to the point where I was tired of having to keep this knowledge to myself and I really wanted to tell someone.

During lunch I told her that I had something really big to tell her. She could tell that I was really worried and that something was playing on my mind.

It's funny because as soon as I came out to her, her response was, 'I know, it's obvious' LOL. For me, this was the best reaction because she already knew; it was obvious to her after being my best friend for so many years. For her to just carry on, laughing as normal, was the best feeling. It was freeing just to be me with her. I didn't have to hide, and I didn't have to watch what I said.

I chose her to come out to during school because not only was she my best friend but we shared a similar experience in school. For her to acknowledge that it wasn't a big deal was just the reassurance that I needed. I look back at this now, and I think having such a great reaction from her was the proof that I needed to know that people out there still loved me. It is what gave me the courage to eventually come out to my family and other friends.

It's really hard to explain in words, but the fact that the weight that I was carrying, almost a burden, just disappeared by simply saying to her 'I'm gay' was liberating. Also, our friendship grew a lot stronger because we could then discuss who we fancied (LOL) but most importantly we had no secrets. I wholeheartedly trusted her, which made our friendship blossom.

I began seeing other people in school have girlfriends, along with other gay people starting to come out. This gave me the courage to stop denying who I was. However, I still wasn't ready to come out to everyone because I was worried about what my family would say if they found out. But I started to tell my friends in school – and if someone bullied me for being gay or asked if I was gay, I didn't deny it; I simply ignored it or made a sarcastic comment back.

In my home life, my family would watch a lot of soaps on TV. I remember that there was a gay guy struggling with his sexuality in one of the shows. I found that eye-opening to witness and watch because I thought, *Oh my God, he understands how I'm feeling.* The fact that my dad watched that with me was a big push for me to start getting ready to come out.

It's weird because the whole time I was hiding who I was, I was very scared of what people would say or that I would get bullied more. But by the time I started coming out to friends, most people had stopped asking if I was gay because the jokes had become old; they'd moved on, and they'd grown up. Also, by this point, when someone was getting bullied, there were a lot more people standing up for the LGBTQIA+ community.

At 17, I had never been more open with my friends, but the complete opposite was true of my relationship with my dad and his girlfriend at the time. I became closed off at home and started arguing a bit more with my dad. Everything felt tense; I felt that I couldn't be who I wanted to be because I was worried I'd disappoint him, and I was very scared of being judged. I simply didn't know how to tell him that I was gay. I didn't want to upset him, and I knew that his girlfriend at the time didn't like gay people. Knowing that his girlfriend was homophobic definitely made it a lot harder to come out, and I think I would have come out to my dad a lot earlier if it weren't for that fact.

We had a great holiday in Blackpool, and he was happy having banter and laughs with drag queens so it made me think he would be okay with me being gay. When I was younger, he would simply buy me all of the girly and feminine things that I wanted, such as the plastic, pink Barbie dolls. He never once judged me or said that I couldn't have the things I wanted. I think that he always knew I was in touch with my feminine side and quite possibly always knew that I was gay – but we never had that conversation.

Then, I got kicked out of home.

One day, he heard from someone in our town that I had told one of my friends that I was gay. During a heated argument, one where we were arguing about something else entirely, he asked me if I was gay. Without thinking, I blurted out, 'Yes, I am gay!' As soon as I said it, I went into shock. I'd admitted it in the heat of the moment, when it wasn't planned and when I wasn't ready.

As soon as the words 'I'm gay' came out, everything kind of slowed down. In all honesty, I don't really remember what happened. We just looked at each other for so long in silence.

I didn't really have a relationship with my mum because, when I was younger, I was put into care due to being mistreated.

Despite having a tough childhood, my dad and I had a strong connection. By not having that mother figure, my dad had to be both, and I feel like in that moment (when I came out) he needed someone else to support him, to make sure he didn't say the wrong thing. Unfortunately, this was not the case, as my dad was dating a homophobic woman.

I truly believe that when you love someone, love is blind; that is simply what happened with my dad.

For the next few days, my dad and I didn't really speak. I think I was still in shock that I'd finally come out to him, the one person I never wanted to disappoint. Ultimately, I didn't want to lose him.

I was stunned over the next few days, and I think Dad was just figuring out what he could say.

In my head, I had always planned to come out when I left home, almost like a fairytale. I couldn't think of telling him face to face, so I thought, *When I go to uni, I'll tell him over text and then I won't have to see his disappointed face.* That being said, even though I had never planned to come out like I did, I had a massive weight lifted off my shoulders. Everyone I cared about now knew I was gay. I was fully out, and there were no more secrets that I had to keep.

Everything that I really didn't want to come true, came true. Over the next few days, after coming out to my dad, his homophobic girlfriend (who'd overheard our conversation) was working her magic on him to try to get me out of the house.

I always knew that it was never my dad's decision. I knew he wasn't homophobic, but he was blind with love for her, and she had control of the house. Ultimately, she got what she wanted. I ended up getting kicked out a few days later – by my dad and her.

I will always remember how some of my clothes were shoved in a black bag, and how I was then chucked out on the street. I was too embarrassed to tell any of my friends, nor did I have any other family members to go to. I honestly didn't know what I was going to do. I was still going to college – I had to travel on a bus that was 40 minutes from where I was living. I'm not necessarily religious, but I was praying, maybe to the universe or whoever could hear me, because it was truly the scariest time of my life.

I ended up sleeping one night on the street – a night that will always stay with me. By this point, I was 17 and had already been in the care system for a year back when I was 13. When I was 14, my dad won custody and I came out of care to live with him full time. However, I knew that 17 was a very difficult time to be in the care system; you're too old to go back into the system but you're also too young to get Housing Association support.

I had so many emotions that night; I was heartbroken that I'd lost my whole family and angry that it was just for me being me. I had lost everything for simply being gay. It didn't make sense to me how people could be so cruel and how this had happened to me. At first, I did regret coming out to my dad, but also, deep down, I was relieved because it meant that there was no more hiding. There was no more reason to fake being someone else; it was finally time for me to live a life that was truly mine. Luckily, finally being able to live as my authentic self made me really happy and has led me to the wonderful life I have now. And I haven't looked back since.

* * *

As our stories show, coming out is not always as easy or straightforward as it should be. But it can be the start of a positive journey to living authentic lives surrounded by those who fully support and embrace you for being you.

♡ Tell or don't tell

That's the big question.

As human beings, we all want to be seen and accepted for who and what we are. However, it can also be scary to open up to our family and friends. And the other thing that many people who are part of the LGBTQIA+ community think is: why should I?

After all, straight teens don't feel any obligation to say, 'Oh, by the way, Mum, I'm straight. Just letting you know!' Or, 'Big news! I feel sexually attracted to the opposite sex – just in case you were wondering!' Why should we have to announce our sexual preferences to people just because they do not comply with the historically straight 'norm'?

It's awkward and embarrassing, right?

Sometimes, as you saw from Matthew's story, the subject just doesn't come up and everyone just goes along not saying anything until it just, well, sorts itself out in its own time and everyone gets used to the idea without rocking the boat one way or the other.

That's fine too, but it can also turn who and what we are as LGBTQIA+ people into the elephant in the room. Or at least it can feel like that.

And let's face it, carrying around the elephant that nobody wants to talk about with you can turn from awkward to heavy after a while.

MATTHEW

> *'Keeping my sexuality a secret took its toll on my mental health.'*

For a while after I came out at school, but not to my family, I found myself living a double life – and that was hard. I have a loving family, but not coming out to them meant that I could not use them to support me through those difficult teenage years when I worried about what was in store for me after I left school, in the next stage of my life. It was a real strain on my mental health, and I worried a lot about whether I'd ever be able to tell my parents. In the end, it worked out absolutely fine, but I wonder if I had opened up earlier whether things might have been easier for me.

♡ Shame is toxic

Silence itself can be painful, especially if it comes from a feeling of shame. People who feel they are 'different' from the rest of the world often start to feel ashamed about it.

Of course, there is *nothing* to feel ashamed about in being LGBTQIA+ (in fact the opposite of shame is 'Pride' and there is a whole chapter on that!)

We can't always control how we feel, but 'shame' is a particularly toxic emotion. Research shows that shame causes people to:

- hide themselves away from community and friendships and never share their true selves with the world
- keep their thoughts and feelings wrapped up tight
- feel worthless, depressed, anxious and suffer from low self-esteem.

Shame contributes to mental health problems such as depression and anxiety. And people who feel shame are less likely to put themselves forward for the jobs and relationships that lead to a full and happy life.

If you don't want to come out because you are feeling ashamed, it is really important to reach out and talk to somebody about your feelings. Do not let them stew! You can find help from some excellent organisations listed in the Resources pages at the end of this book.

Now, you might feel such relief that you finally get to be your authentic, true self that you want to shout it from the rooftops and post an Instagram story or TikTok video.

But most of us aren't that brave! You might be thinking about how your world could change if you share your identity difference with others. How will others react? Will your parents be surprised, shocked, disappointed? Friends could be dismissive – or bitchy? What if word spreads to someone you'd prefer didn't know? Or the whole school?

The bottom line is: Is it safe for me to disclose?

♡ Why come out/invite in?

There are all kinds of reasons you might want or feel the need to disclose your sexuality/gender identity.

- I am ready to start dating, and I want my family members and close friends to know that.
- I like who I am, and I am sick of hearing people around me using stereotypes and negative labels about a group I am a part of.
- I feel as if I'm hiding a part of myself away, as if I am living a lie and not being fully myself out in the world.
- I want to feel accepted and respected for who I truly am. I've met someone and want to be able to share my love openly and not hide our relationship.

♡ Choosing not to come out/invite in

Like we said, disclosing this information about yourself is not compulsory or a given. It depends on each individual's wants and needs – and their beliefs about who they are and who they want to be perceived as.

That aside, sometimes there are very practical reasons for *not* 'coming out' that you should consider before making this decision.

- I am part of a closed community that is not accepting of LGBTQIA+ people, or I am part of a family/religious group where my sexuality would be frowned on.

- I am afraid that I will face bullying, harassment, discrimination or even violence.
- My families, friends or community don't know, and I am worried about what might happen if people find out 'the truth'.
- I'm not yet sure about who I am or how I feel. I don't want to 'come out' until I have fully figured things out for myself.

♡ The right decision for your circumstance

Let's be really honest here – they are all super-valid reasons for coming out and not coming out, but there are a few things definitely worth considering.

If you are still living with your parents and dependent on them or other adults for your care and well-being, disclosing that information can be complicated.

If you live in a situation or a place where being LGBTQIA+ is accepted, you are more likely to get support from family and friends. It's different for everyone, so it's really important that before you do anything, you carefully consider your situation. It's important that you feel safe. Ensure that the environment you're in is a space where you feel secure. Maybe that means waiting until your home is quiet and less busy, or choosing to do it outside your house in a coffee shop or during a walk in the park.

However, not everyone needs to make a 'moment' out of it. Many people come out gradually. They start off by telling a school counsellor or maybe one close family member, or a friend who they know is accepting of LGBTQIA+ people. If you want to be sure your information stays completely private, don't be afraid to start by calling an LGBTQIA+ support line. **You will find a list of them in our Resources section.** A lot of people choose to go to a support group before telling their loved ones, so that they can have help and support working through their feelings about identity or coming out to their family and friends.

♡ Be prepared

Coming out is a big and personal decision, and there is no way to really know how the people in your life will react until the time comes.

However, you can think ahead and start looking for clues about how people think. Ask them to watch popular TV shows like *RuPaul's Drag Race* or *Heartstopper* and start to see where they stand on gay culture. Bring up LGBTQIA+ issues in conversation. What do they think about what's happening with same-gender marriage in America and churches having the right not to marry same-gender couples based on their right to freedom of religion? Are they disapproving and negative, or are they open-minded and accepting of same-gender marriage?

Even when you think someone might react positively to your news, there's still no guarantee. Everyone responds based on their own situations. Parents who accept an LGBTQIA+ friend may be upset when their own child comes out. It could be because they worry their child might face discrimination. Or it could be they struggle with beliefs that being LGBTQIA+ is wrong.

Below are some things to keep in mind when you're thinking of coming out.

What does your gut tell you?
Coming out is a process. Different people are ready for it at different times in their lives. Never feel forced to come out by friends or situations. You might want to be open about who you are, but it's crucial you think about your own safety first. If you think there is a risk that you could be physically harmed or thrown out of your home, it's probably safer not to share. Instead, call a helpline like the LGBT Foundation Helpline for advice and support.

Manage your expectations
We all go into these situations hoping for a good outcome. However, people you come out to might not react the way you want or expect them to. You might think your best friend will be super cool – but they might get a fright and react badly. You might think your parents will be horrified and then they say, 'Oh we already knew' (which is meant well but can be frustrating to hear!). Some relationships take time to settle back to what they were. Some might change permanently. Friends and family – even the most supportive people – may need time to get used to the idea. After all, this is big news for you, so it's going to be big news for your loved ones too. Put yourself in the other person's shoes. As much as you are adjusting to these feelings, sometimes parents need space to transition too. Needing space to process your news isn't necessarily a negative reaction, but adjusting to 'the new normal' can be a journey for your loved ones too.

Create a support system

Explore the connections you have and decide if there is a friend or grown-up you trust enough to tell. But if you can't talk openly about your identity, the online community is an amazing place to meet and connect with others. It can help you build supportive friendships, and you can use social media platforms to stay connected – and to simply find your tribe. This is one of the reasons why we post content, especially around LGBTQIA+ topics, and why we go live on our social media channels to offer support to those who need it. We want to remind people that we're all one big community – there's so much love online and creators, including ourselves, who will welcome you into their online family.

Or if you're trying to figure out if you should come out, don't be afraid to pick up the phone or go online for help. There are tons of other people in your boat – no matter how bad things are, you are not alone. There is always hope and help.

Having these support systems in place can help you plan how to come out (or not). They can also help you cope if any reactions to your coming out lead to you needing practical help, even shelter. As we know from our own experience, even when things are really bad there is always help there, and hope is just around the corner.

Peer pressure and privacy

Historically, to become part of our culture, LGBTQIA+ people either had to come out and declare themselves or stay 'hidden in the closet'. That was before LGBTQIA+ people were as visible and outspoken as they are today. Some people in the LGBTQIA+ community feel that there is still too much pressure to 'come out' – and we agree. Everyone has the right to privacy, and nobody should feel obliged to 'come out' and declare their sexual orientation or gender identity.

Peer pressure can also come from friends. Friends might be declaring their own sexuality, telling you who they like, who they are into and wanting you to share back.

You absolutely do not have to do the same. Coming out/inviting in is YOUR decision. Just yours! Even if other people you know have come out or if you've told some people but not others, no one has a say in when or how you disclose the information or who you disclose it to. *You* are in charge of how and when you do it. It's nobody else's business. You might have friends who are mature enough to respect your personal, private information, but whenever you share information there's a risk it could leak to people you might not want to know, so think it through beforehand. That's why sometimes using a helpline or counselling service first can work because therapists and counsellors are required to keep any information you share private.

It can be a lifelong process
Coming out is a lifelong process. You will make new friends and family, meet new partners and join new companies throughout your life. So you may have to come out again in new situations. The good news is – being LGBTQIA+ does not have the stigma it used to have, and the more of us that can stand up and live our lives publicly with pride, the better.

However, depending on the situation you are living in, that is not always possible. Weigh things up in terms of your own life and consider the pros and cons of whether you should come out. Are you in a safe environment? Always put your safety and well-being first. Is there a person/people you can trust? They're important for you to have as support and confide in. Would the response of the person you tell be definitively negative? Perhaps it's better they don't know for now. Would you feel better afterwards? Listen to what your gut is telling you, and, once thought out, do what feels right to you.

True Life Story: I proudly exist as an LGBT+ Muslim

Rayyan Aboobaker (he/they) shares their experience of being a bisexual and transgender non-binary Muslim.

Figuring my way through my faith and identity was a rollercoaster.

Being an LGBT+ Muslim comes with its hardships and struggles. Being gay, bisexual or transgender can be difficult in general, but when you come from a traditional cultural background, you also have to deal with homophobia/transphobia as well as Islamophobia from various communities. Being afraid of rejection from loved ones for simply being yourself is one of the hardest experiences a person can have.

I realised I was different when I was a young child, around four or five years old, but I didn't have the words to describe it until I was around 17. From early childhood to my teenage years, I was told to be the daughter my family wanted me to be, but to me, that felt wrong. I didn't consider myself a girl, but because I didn't understand who I was I lied to myself and chased happiness that wasn't my own.

I despised who I was, and self-hatred fuelled my mind and convinced me that I didn't deserve to be happy. This was amplified by the constant 'why can't you be like every girl?' from my mum and my prayers for my mother's wish to come true.

I built walls around myself, became isolated and refused to talk about the conflict inside me where I thought I had to choose between my faith and identity since being LGBT+ and Muslim seemed like two separate worlds that could never coincide with each other.

Until one day everything changed. I met a new friend – a Brown, gay man who came from a faith background. Meeting him broke every belief I had had about myself. I realised, in that moment, that I wasn't alone. I wasn't the only one. And neither are you.

His confidence helped me break down every inch of my walls. His kindness supported me in my exploration of my identity. His big-heartedness built my confidence to attend Trans Pride in London for the first time. His friendship is the reason I am who I am today.

He encouraged me to learn more about Islam and its call for social justice. I learned that my religion has always been tolerant of diversity. Despite Islam sometimes being used to oppress LGBT+ groups, I discovered that the true meaning of Islam is actually peace and acceptance of everyone.

Today, I proudly exist as an LGBT+ Muslim. I am a volunteer with Just Like Us, the LGBT+ young people's charity, where I speak to young people about my experiences. To be able to give younger generations the education and representation I never had at their age is so important because no one should feel the fear and shame I went through. I hope all young LGBT+ Muslims feel pride in themselves. And even if you don't see yourself represented right now, you could one day be that representation for someone else.

I still feel afraid of being rejected and sometimes guilty for being myself, but having come out to my closest friends and my best friend in my life I know I will always be loved, even when I don't want to accept it.

Remember that when everything seems so dark, there is someone who loves you and will always love you for who you are.

Matthew and Ryan's Top 12 Tips for Coming Out/ Inviting In

1. First, know that you aren't required to 'come out'. It is your decision whether you tell people or not.
2. If you decide to come out, weigh up each possible scenario that could unfold and decide if you're prepared to deal with the consequences of what could be.
3. Keep in mind that it doesn't have to be a serious or scary thing. The moment can be as lighthearted as you make it.
4. Practise what you want to say before you have the conversation.
5. Decide on *where* you are going to come out. Find a place where you feel comfortable and safe.

6. Remember that you know yourself better than anyone else does; don't let others make you doubt what you know to be true.
7. It's really helpful if you have somebody you can turn to and chat with for support before and after you have any big conversations: a friend, a family member, or an LGBTQIA+ guidance counsellor.
8. You might also need to have another person with you, like a supportive friend, when you are coming out to others.
9. Don't expect the conversation to go perfectly smoothly – especially if you're coming out to older people – allow them the grace to ask ignorant questions so long as they're not being hurtful.
10. If someone doesn't take your coming out well, allow them time to process. Older people, in particular, often need space to come to terms with who you truly are versus the idea they have of who you are.
11. With that said, don't be afraid to address people's incorrect assumptions or misinformed responses.
12. Lastly, we want you to know that – no matter what! – we love you, and you will always have a family here with us.

The Matthew Truth

There is no right or wrong way of coming out.

I've never *actually* told my dad that I'm gay.

We're both quite similar in terms of being lighthearted jokesters, so back then we were either making jokes and having laughs or, being the typical dad, he would help me with things like decorating my room or putting something complicated together. Me being gay was a serious topic, and I wasn't sure how to broach the conversation at the time. In the end, I just assumed that my mum would tell him, and, of course, he now knows I live an openly gay life and have a long-term boyfriend. I never 'officially' came out to my whole family, and while I sometimes might wish I had done things differently, the most important thing is that it all worked out in the end. Being true to yourself is crucial, and whatever steps you do or don't take to show yourself to the world, life has a way of honouring the true you – as it did with me and my family.

RYAN RECOMMENDS

Ignore people who say 'it's a phase'.

You might know you like girls or boys – then share it with someone and they say, 'Oh, it might just be a phase' or 'You're too young to know.'

This is *so* dismissive. The idea of sexual orientation being a 'phase' diminishes the person who is sharing that confidence. Also, it doesn't matter if it is or isn't a phase. No one knows your journey, no one knows how you're feeling, and no one has the right to label your feelings as a phase. Exploring your sexuality, being who you want to be, trying different things is part of the process of self-discovery. Never put pressure on yourself to get past 'a phase' because you just don't know. Even if you're in your twenties, thirties, forties, fifties, sixties, you might start having feelings for the same sex. Nothing that happens to your feelings should be dismissed. Falling in love is never a blip, it just means that you're finding yourself. People change all the time, at any age. It's okay to change. You can be whoever you want to be, whenever you want to be it.

♡ Being outed! Personal advice

You pick up your phone one morning, and it's flooded with nasty messages. You kiss your secret crush, and somebody takes a picture and posts it online. You confide in a friend, but they tell their mum, and she tells your mum and next thing, everybody knows your secret. Being outed, deliberately or even by accident, is terrible. If this has happened to you the first thing we want to say is, we are so sorry. Somebody 'outing' you is just completely unacceptable behaviour. As we have said, it is your decision to bring people in by sharing this information about yourself. It's not for somebody else to push this out into the world. Whether it's somebody you have told who betrayed your confidence, or just that people are talking and making assumptions, it is a hurtful experience. However, if it does happen to you – here's our personal advice.

Ryan: Get to grips with the situation as quickly as possible and decide what you want to do. You've still got time to take things into your own hands. If you want to tell people and have been putting it off, tell the people you most want to know first – that way you could own the situation as a way to come out and just ride the wave. And if you really don't want to do that, there is no shame in just backtracking. Say it's not true and wait until you are ready. It's hard enough to come out on your own, but if you're forced to come out it can be even tougher, and you don't owe anyone this information about yourself.

Matthew: I agree. Even though it is awful being 'outed' it can sometimes be a good way of really knowing people's reactions. You can backtrack if this is possible, but sometimes it won't be. If that's the case, you should try to deal with. But it's important that you *really* remember who *you* are and don't get stressed over everyone else's opinions. If people are negative, it's not a reflection of you. It's their problem, not yours.

Ryan: And you don't have to do it on your own. There is a big community of people out there (like us!) who will support you if you are the victim of a malicious outing. And again, you might not be ready, and that's absolutely okay. As I said, there is no shame in backtracking. It doesn't mean you are not a proud LGBTQIA+ person – it just means you deserve to choose to tell people when and if you feel ready.

JUST LIKE US, the LGBT+ young people's charity have shared some really useful advice on how to stay safe when coming out:

1. If you're thinking about coming out, put yourself first. You don't owe anyone an explanation, and you should never be pressured to tell anyone how you identify.
2. Get support. Switchboard is a LGBT+ helpline. It has an online chat and phone helpline where you can speak to someone LGBT+ for confidential support. It has lots of useful information and will listen to anything you'd like to chat to them about.
3. Safety first – is there someone you trust who you know will likely be an ally if you were to come out to them? Start with someone supportive if you do want to come out.
4. There is no rush – you can take all the time you need. Some people don't come out until they're an adult or much older, others come out very young. Everyone is on their own journey and pace. Do what is right for you.
5. Coming out can be overrated! Yes, really. It's not a necessary part of being LGBT+, and sharing that part of your identity isn't something you owe anyone. Sharing that part of you with someone is a gift – you should never feel rushed or pressured to come out.

6. Coming out is rarely a one-time thing. LGBT+ people come out in lots of ways – at work, with new friends, when they go to new places. It's something that LGBT+ people can choose to share with different people in different areas of their life, throughout their lifetime.
7. The most important thing is coming out to yourself. Take your time to figure out how you feel, what words best describe your identity (perhaps there isn't one yet!) and what support you need.
8. Be a good ally to others coming out too. Think about how your actions might make others feel, and if someone comes out to you, make sure you ask for permission before sharing that with anyone else. If anyone wants to share something about you online or in real life that you're not happy with, you have the right to say no too.

Matthew & Ryan chat with...

Roxanne Weijer, **lesbian**, and her other half, Maartje Hensen, **bi. Together they are @onceuponajourney**

M&R: Can you describe your journey of coming out or finding your identity?

Roxanne: I'm fortunate and privileged to come from one of the most welcoming countries in the world, the Netherlands. Still, coming out wasn't easy. Or it didn't feel easy.

I struggled finding myself and coming out, as society is (still) made for straight people. My parents and siblings expected me to come home with a man. And I kissed boys during high school and while studying because that felt the way to go.

Everything changed when I met my girlfriend Maartje and when I started going to a student association with many queer people. Being surrounded by these people, I realised I wasn't straight.

I fell in love with Maartje, and after being together for a few weeks, I knew I had to tell people about our relationship, though I was afraid. Afraid to be different, afraid to be rejected.

Maartje had already told her whole family, and I needed a little push to tell mine too. For some family members, my lesbian coming out was a big surprise. And some people, like my mom, had to get used to it. The first thing she told me was, 'It's better than seeing two guys kissing.' Yikes!

M&R: Do you have any advice for someone struggling with their identity?

Take your time to figure out who you are and what your identity is.

Identities and sexuality can be fluid too – don't rush 'labelling' yourself. Don't push yourself too hard. It is your timeline; you do not have to figure it out within a set amount of time. It is okay to be confused; that's part of the process.

And it is good to know, it is *not* mandatory to come out. You don't owe it to anyone to disclose your sexual and/or gender identity if you don't want to.

Coming out can be really scary, so take your time. And when you are ready, come out to a friend or person that you really trust, a person that you know will accept you no matter what. And/or find like-minded people online.

Then give the people you came out to time, too. You took your time to figure out who you are, let them take time as well. I needed a little push to come out, but it's really important to take your time!

♡ The last word on inviting in

> *'Everyone's journey is different, and there is no rush to "come out" or invite in. Take time to think about what's right for you.'* Matthew and Ryan

Rainbow Stories: Inviting In
Our Rainbow World **Community** share their stories:

Fin, 20, he/him, homosexual

I never really 'came out'. When talking to people in school, I would never say if I found someone attractive, and, for the most part, I avoided talking about what boys or girls were hot. I just never spoke freely about anything like that or about my attraction to do with either side, so people just didn't know. Then eventually, I started seeing a boy from the town over, and that's how everyone happened to find out. To be honest, I think everyone kind of knew anyway.

A few years after that, my mom 'found out' when I was in my first semester of college (even though I'd been openly bringing my secondary school boyfriend home the months we were together). On a weekend trip home from college, we were in the kitchen making dinner together, and she asked if I was with anyone. I hinted at a 'maybe', and she simply asked me, 'A boy or girl?' I said, 'A boy' and that's all there was to it. Now, whenever it happens to come up, it's a natural part of our conversations.

Kelly, 26, she/her, questioning/queer

My coming out to my nearest and dearest was a series of amusingly heartfelt disclosures over three consecutive days.

Day 1: Out with three friends, pizza arrives, one sentence rushing to the surface: 'I like girls and boys. I'm bi.' Loose grins, my relieved breath and their excited squeals, followed by 'Let's celebrate!'

Day 2: Movie sleepover with two other friends – fluffy socks and anxiety. Time to do it all over again. We're on the phone with a friend from the night before: 'Have you told them yet?' 'No, not yet.' 'Oh, sorry.' Taking the handheld opportunity, I go with it. 'I'm bisexual.' 'I thought you were gonna say you were preggers, thank god.' A round of bone-crushing hugs and a big conversation about what we would've done if I was pregnant.

Day 3: AKA Pancake Tuesday; coming out to my mum was like defeating the Big Boss at the end of a video game; this is what it had all been leading to. In the car park of Tesco: she was sitting behind the wheel, me in the passenger seat, both of us waiting for my younger brother to return with a bottle of ready-made pancake mix. On a roll of validated hope from my friends' definitive acceptance, I was too optimistic when it came to my Catholic mother. 'I have something to tell you.' 'Don't tell me you're pregnant.' 'No, I'm bi, bisexual... I like girls and boys.' 'Oh, weird.' Defensive: 'What's weird about it?' 'I don't know... I get liking one or the other, but both?' I had been naively hoping for more squeals and hugs but instead my brother returned to find the both of us sitting in uncomfortable silence, me staring melancholically out the car window and Mum at a loss for words.

(It's got way better since then! Give the older generation time to process, and if they can get past the ideologies they grew up with they will accept your true self.)

Whitney and Megan Bacon-Evans, lesbian couple, content creators/activists, @whatwegandidnext

We both knew we were gay from a young age and both came out around age 15–16 years old and had similar experiences with our mums reacting badly. However, we were actually in completely different countries at the time! Whitney grew up in a small religious town in Kentucky, and it was particularly hard for her, with the high school experience of being bullied. She knew she would have to leave the South in order to become the person she was meant to be, so she studied her degree in Hawaii and then moved to join Megan in the UK in

2012. Helping people with their identity/sexuality, we would advise confiding in people who you know will be supportive, or finding a community – online is great for this! For those struggling to come out from fear of losing friends, if you go online and reach out to the active community you will build new friendships with like-minded people.

Mary, 21, she/her, bisexual

I had a sort of 'coming out' in third year. One of the girls in my friendship group had recently come out, and I felt that, because someone else had said it, it would be the ideal time for me too. I didn't think I had to come out, but I figured that if this information needed to be said, I needed to say it. Despite that, I still thought it was a massive deal because I thought that nobody knew. I remember that it was during lunch break, and we were all at our lunch spot, sitting on tables, chilling. I'd hyped myself up so much for it, and I finally said, 'Okay lads, I'm bi', and they just said, 'We already knew.' And then we just laughed and ate lunch. It was so calm.

Taylor, 21, they/them, lesbian

My coming out was a long time coming and significantly less dramatic than I think I had earned, but nevertheless it happened, and it happened all because I got sat beside a 12-year-old bisexual on my first day of secondary school orientation. There's so little to tell about this part of my queer journey because it was so anticlimactic, but I think, looking back, that was a good thing. Dare I say, it might have even been the point because when the bisexual told me what they identified as and why, what that meant and how they felt, then turned the mic to me, all of a sudden I had all the exact same things to say.

It wasn't like a light switch. It wasn't a moment of realisation but rather like a small weight had been plucked off of my back. The bisexual barely reacted, just nodded their acknowledgment and went about their day, unaware that they had normalised something that had existed within me in terrified scorn for the majority of my life.

Frances, 22, he/him, they/them, homosexual

Coming out can feel so exhausting and endless. To the innocent, one might think it's a week-long affair of telling your classmates or colleagues about an intimate part of yourself. The responses are expected to be either moving or brutal. I think it's the length of coming out that exhausts most people: in school, and again in college, in every job you begin, most doctor appointments, parties, nights out, holidays – until the end of time. But there is also the option to not partake in any of it. Move through the world as your truest self without any labels or agenda, and kiss whoever you like. I never had the choice of coming out – I kissed a boy who (very kindly) told everyone we mutually knew. And that was that, before I even had my mind made up.

Kelly, 23, she/her, trans lesbian

I was outed before I was ready to say anything.

A lot of coming out, I've had no control over. With my family, I was outed before I was ready to say anything. With friends, at least I had some control, but that was clumsy too. With people from home, it's awkward, I'm not really sure who knows or who doesn't at this stage. With friends in college, it was easier. I could just change my name on social media. Things might have been easier if I hadn't purged older social media accounts I had people from home on.

Things my parents said when they found out still stick with me. That they were traumatised. That they were losing a son. That I wouldn't have the confidence to go through with this. That no woman would love me. That my siblings would be bullied because of me. That my little brother – nine at the time – wouldn't be able to understand. That it would simply break his brain. (It didn't. He understood better than any of them.) Maybe I didn't have much confidence, but it sure would have been easier to have more support.

With my friends – a small circle at this point – I mentioned using she/her pronouns in one conversation. At first some used them, but when a few months passed nobody was doing it, and I didn't have the confidence to correct them. I'd make self-deprecating jokes to remind them I was still a trans woman, but that didn't work either. I hadn't told them my name because I was still scared. And knew that it would hurt much more to have that ignored. When I did tell them nobody used it, and it really did hurt. I couldn't answer their messages for a few days but also didn't have the strength to say what was wrong. Fed up, I re-entered the group chat with a new account that said Ciara and came out to everyone else in college.

My friends have never slipped up since – I can't say I hold a grudge really. It did hurt, and I nearly stopped talking to them entirely, but I have to take some blame too for not asserting myself

LOVE IS LOVE MOMENT:
Determined to win

Ryan can get very competitive. He's always there to win; if he wants to achieve something he's got to go do it. Ryan doesn't give up!
Malcolm, Ryan's dad

LOVE IS LOVE MOMENT:
Pints of poop

One day, many years ago, we both went out for a couple of drinks after work. Ryan's drink got pooped in by a bird, and the bar wouldn't let him get a replacement!
Samara, friend

CHAPTER 4
Living with Pride

Pride is how we live our life and how we celebrate our community.

We've all seen the marches on TV and the rainbow flag, but 'Pride' is so much more than that. For us, it's about being your authentic true self and being comfortable with who you are.

Until now, we've been talking through discovering yourself, figuring things out, coming out or not coming out. Living with Pride is what all that tough stuff leads to. Feeling proud in yourself, as an LGBTQIA+ person, and living your life – *however you choose.*

That's important, because not everyone wants to go to marches, or watch drag shows and wave rainbow flags (although all of these things are fun!). You can have an LGBTQIA+ identity and simply just carry on pursuing the same interests you have always had – gaming, dancing, football, music, fashion. We are Matthew and Ryan, Pokémon fans, pranksters, travellers – we just also happen to be gay. You may have heard the saying 'Loud and Proud' before. But you can be proud without being loud! LGBTQIA+ Pride is primarily about us as individuals claiming the fact that we are happy and comfortable in our orientation and identity. That we are not ashamed. And that is so important.

Pride is the way LGBTQIA+ people stand our ground as equal members of society. It's the bedrock on which we build our lives and our community in a world which is – frankly – not always as accepting as it should be.

And for us, it's not just politics – it's personal. Learning to live with Pride helped us hold our heads higher, and it strengthened us through our personal hardships.

RYAN: FINDING HAPPINESS

The night I was kicked out of my home for being gay gave me a lot to reflect on, and it made me think about how I wanted to live my life. Ultimately, it kind of started a fire within my soul. I was determined to continue my studies at college and make a life for myself on my own, while being my authentic self.

After that night sleeping on the street, I headed to college and explained to some of my friends what had happened. I was fortunate that one of my friends and her family said they would put me up while I was on a waiting list to move into a hostel. During this period, for the first time in my life I felt free. I bleached my hair white-blonde, I got a nose ring, and I got a tattoo. I'm not gonna lie, I went through a bit of a rebellious phase.

After I left my friend's house I moved into a hostel. This was the hardest time of my life. It nearly pushed me to breaking point. I kept myself to myself and just focused on my studies to make sure that I got good grades so that I could finally go to university and start a fresh, new life for myself. While everyone around me was going home for family meals on a Sunday, I was in my hostel room alone. I had to learn how to cook, clean, sort out my own bills and, well, grow up.

However, during this year, I really took control of my life and my independence. I actually started dating, which was so exciting! For the first time I wasn't ashamed of who I was.

When I tell people my coming-out story, some ask if I could go back now, would I still come out knowing that I was going to get kicked out and be isolated from my family?

And I say, without getting kicked out, I would still be living as a shadow of myself and worried about my dad's opinion of me.

Being kicked out of home and having no one to answer to, having no family members to impress with what you're saying and doing, and simply not having to put up a fight over how you want to live your life, means that you purely and solely focus on yourself. I finally got a voice.

So, no, I don't regret coming out. I don't regret the hard stuff that I had to face because it wouldn't have made me the person I am today. It wouldn't have pushed me to go to university, which ultimately led me to the crazy, amazing life I have now with my soulmate Matthew. The experience that I went through taught me how to be independent and strong and how I can do anything I want to do if I put my mind to it.

Being kicked out also taught me not to sweat the small stuff. It taught me about forgiveness and how everyone makes mistakes. I know my dad's heart was in the best place, and I know that he was blinded by love for his girlfriend at the time it happened. Time has passed, mistakes have been healed and apologies have been made. Me and Dad have a great relationship today. He accepts me for who I am.

Everything that happened in the past led me to the amazing family that I have now with Matthew and Roscoe, and the wonderful online community we share. I am proud of my life today – and I am proud of all I went through to get here.

EVERYDAY SCENARIOS

As a gay couple, just living our lives, we often find ourselves in situations that straight people just don't have to deal with. One of the challenges of Pride is how you hold yourself in these situations. Making ourselves visible helps further the normalising of same-gender couples in society; however, sometimes it can be a bit of a tightrope!

Here are a few of the everyday scenarios we come up against.

♡ Everyday scenario: Genuine mistake

Hotel receptionist: 'Oh, there must be a mistake, you've booked a double room instead of two singles?'

Sometimes people are coming from a place of genuine inexperience of LGBTQIA+ people and subsequent lack of knowledge about the protocol, and in general their mistakes are genuine. But they can be annoying.

Matthew, warm smile: 'Actually, we're a couple. A double is fine.'

The receptionist should understand that you are not offended or angry, that you know it was a genuine mistake, but that she might be more careful in jumping to conclusions next time a same-gender couple books in. On the other hand, she might be more insistent and be a bit snarky about it. When you are travelling, it's important to be sensitive to your surroundings, for instance, when you are travelling through a conservative part of the United States, or a foreign country where LGBTQIA+ rights and issues are not recognised or even criminalised. If this is the case, don't bother fighting. It's not worth it and might actually be unsafe.

♡ Everyday scenario: Well-meaning assumptions

Elderly aunt: Have you got a girlfriend?

Sometimes old relatives and family friends are genuinely curious and just being sweet. But sometimes they are digging for information that is none of their business.

Matthew: Ah, Auntie, I actually have a boyfriend.

If she looks horrified and seems disapproving or even not at all receptive to this information, it might be better to laugh it off and say you're focusing on yourself.

However, if she smiles, asks you about your partner and invites you to explain further, you might have found yourself an elderly ally!

♡ Everyday scenario: The toilets

Mens? Ladies? What about us?

There is so much unnecessary discomfort for LGBTQIA+ people around gendered bathrooms. Trans men and women especially are often made to feel uncomfortable about sharing a bathroom with other people of their gender.

The politics of male and female toilets is a big gender rights community issue because it comes down the most basic of human needs – somewhere safe to do your business!

Ryan: As a man who wears make-up, I just hate going into the men's toilets. Especially if we are out on a date and it's a busy restaurant at the weekend, so I know the bathroom will be packed. Lots of men I don't know in that confined space – it just feels very threatening.

Matthew: I love when we are both all dressed up and Ryan has got his full face on. It's a disappointment, though, when the perfect evening is interrupted by something as basic as using the toilet. Of course, I am always happy to accompany him in.

Ryan: And sometimes I will use the disabled toilets.

Matthew: But it's still not good enough. Small steps like asking if they have gender-neutral toilets before booking somewhere send a message to establishments that the LGBTQIA+ community mean business. ***In the meantime, always bring a friend in with you if you feel nervous.***

♡ Everyday scenario: Straight Pride

Straight friend: Why do gay people get a Pride and straight people don't?

Some people think that because LGBTQIA+ people are more visible we now have equal rights to straight people, but we still have a long way to go on this front. So it's important to make this clear!

Do you get bullied for being straight? Er, no. ***Okay, are you discriminated against for being straight? Is it illegal to be straight in over 70 countries?*** I don't think so, no? ***Correct. And are you banned from marrying the person you love? Do you and your girlfriend get harassed or worried that you're going to get attacked in the streets for showing each other love?*** Definitely not.

So, that's why you don't need a straight Pride. You have rights! Ah, okay. Now I get it!

Most people do, to be honest. Sometimes people just need to have things explained to them. And you can always let them know that cis straight people can always join the party as supporters of their LGBTQIA+ community. Allies are a valued part of our community too!

Matthew and Ryan's Tips to Live Everyday Life with Pride

- Pride means being your authentic true self. Wear what you want, talk how you want – *be* who you are in the world and be happy with it.
- Even if people don't agree with it or if you get snarky comments from people, don't let them get to you. After all, it's their problem, not yours.
- Celebrate the small everyday things, like the things you're grateful for in your life and the people you love. Don't change yourself just to fit in. We are all unique;

no one should need to conform for others. Be yourself, unapologetically, every day.
- During Pride Month, you can dress up and join Pride marches. There is no obligation, but it is more fun than you could ever imagine. If you feel comfortable and feel like attending, it's a great way to meet people and make friends for life!
- Join LGBTQIA+ societies in your school, university or local community, and help other young people who might be struggling with their identity. Be part of change by volunteering for projects like Queer Futures, a study on LGBTQ mental health.
- Advocate and stand up for the people in our community, particularly our trans brothers and sisters, who are still denied some basic gender rights and life-affirming social acceptance.

Live every day with pride by being proud of who you are and proud to be a part of a community who continue to fight for our rights

♡ Proud posse!

Since we both came out and began to live our life together, we have made friends in the LGBTQIA+ online community – so many amazing people from all over the world leading different lives, but all of us have one thing in common: Pride!

Cole
@coleandabbie

Pride for me is a place to feel fearless. A place to reflect on all those years of hurt, to stand and make a change.

Richard and Lewis
@twodadsinlondon

Pride means being able to love who you are and show an equal love to others who may be different, because wouldn't it be boring if we were all the same?! It's a celebration of who you are and being proud to share that with everyone, especially those who are also different.

Whitney
@whatwegandidnext

Pride is something me and my wife Megan feel 24/7, 365 days of the year. We're proud to be lesbians, wife and wife, and part of the LGBTQ+ community.

Roxanne
@onceuponajourney

Pride means so much to me; it's a moment to celebrate but also a moment to protest.

Pride is a moment to celebrate how far we've come and how proud we can be (in certain places). It's a protest as homosexuality is still illegal in over 79 countries. There's still so much work to do. There have been incredible queer people fighting the battle long before us. We owe it to them to show our pride and continue to fight for equality!

My girlfriend and I are proud every single day of the year, but not everyone can be out and proud yet. Visibility matters; with visibility, boldness, authenticity and pride come acceptance and progress.

I love how in places like Amsterdam (our home town) we have the amazing canal parade as a party and celebration, but also a Pride walk as a protest. Some people seem to forget that Pride is still a protest, and when they only come to party, we also highly encourage them to come to the protest.

True Life Story: Pride Is Feeling Confident in Myself as a Trans

For a long time, I feared looking like a transphobic caricature. The 'man in a dress' that cis people love to laugh about. As time goes on, I care less and less. I'm a lot more confident in myself and present as feminine a lot more often. I always felt so detached from my body and from fashion, but now it's something I put effort into that feels much more rewarding. Not that I don't still struggle with dysphoria. There are a lot of things I'm insecure about, like any other woman, cis or trans. With time, though, it's becoming manageable. I really do like how I look now. I can believe other people if they tell me I look nice.

Starting hormone replacement therapy was a big deal for me too. I've been on it for eight months now. It can be slow, but going on it was the best decision of my life. It's hard to describe to anyone who hasn't been through it. The cloud just lifts. You start to realise things about yourself you could never see with it there. You become more in tune with your emotions. Your body changes with you. To anyone who would tell me I'm stuck with a 'male body' – whatever that means – I can only laugh. We do have the ability to change our own bodies, and you'll have to deal with that. Sometimes in subtle ways. It took someone else pointing it out for me to realise that my face looks a lot more feminine now, that my cheeks have filled out a bit more – sometimes in ways that are difficult to hide.

And that can be scary. But now I'm done with hiding!

♡ Sharing our Rainbow World

We hope you're now ready to live a life of Pride. The good news is – you have a whole support network out there. Not just in friends but in history, art, culture, politics and celebrity culture. LGBTQIA+ lives are rich and fulfilling, and despite obstacles put in front of us, historically we have contributed to science, politics, culture and art for centuries!

Here are some things about our history and culture we should all be truly proud of!

Five reasons why it's great to be LGBTQIA+:

1. We are part of a global community without borders. There is a sense of unity and strength because we stand together. There are *a lot* of us out there, and we can now connect with everyone through social media.
2. We are part of a historical, political movement. Stand up and be counted – we have made change happen. And we are still fighting strong today.

3. We appreciate beauty and difference in others and ourselves. People in our community are often inclined to be empathetic, passionate and creative.
4. We are cultural influencers. Our community has always been on the cutting edge of modernism. From queer influence on the fashion industry to the rising popularity of drag queens in mainstream media, our community's influence on the arts is profound. Things are forever changing and FAST – we are part of that.
5. We can make our own family. So many LGBTQIA+ people from around the world have been rejected by their families for not conforming to religious or social norms. For this reason, our community is especially good at creating our own families from friends and allies. Our community has always been one of kinship and found family.

♡ Pride Movement: Some facts

In order for us to enjoy the present, it is important to look back too: to inform ourselves and understand where we have come from and how WE HAVE COME SO FAR!

- Pride, across continents, individually and over decades, began as a protest.
- The renowned Stonewall Riots in the USA – the protest that was the catalyst for American Pride and made waves globally – involved nearly 400 people and continued for

- six nights straight. They sparked a movement of LGBT political activism.
- Today, LGBTQIA+ people can be seen everywhere, from YouTubers to politicians, from professional athletes to movie stars.
- The very first Pride Flag was created by Gilbert Baker who was tasked with fabricating a new 'gay' symbol in place of the pink triangle – because the Nazis forced gay men to wear them in concentration camps. The Pride Flag was created in 1978.
- The original Pride Flag featured eight colours, each with its own meaning. Red symbolises life, orange represents healing, pink portrays sexuality, yellow stands for sunlight, green depicts nature, turquoise represents creativity, indigo displays harmony and violet illustrates spirit. The flag was later simplified to six colours; removing the indistinct turquoise, and the hot pink as the fabric was too hard to find.
- The latest update of the community banner is being called the Progress Pride Flag. It includes the colours black and brown to represent people of colour, and, to represent trans people, the colours pink, baby blue and white. These new colours are placed beside the old, in the triangular shape of an arrow, to highlight the progress that is yet to be achieved.
- In the UK, we celebrate LGBT History Month in February. This is to commemorate the end of Section 28, which was a law that banned homosexuality from being discussed in schools.

- However, the USA, Canada and Australia celebrate LGBT History Month in October. This month includes National Coming Out Day on 11 October, which is a day dedicated to helping LGBT people express who they are while feeling comfortable and supported.
- There are over 50 flags created to represent different factions of the LGBTQIA+ community.
- Since 16 November 2015, same-gender couples can legally get married in Ireland. Ireland, a deeply Catholic country, was the first country to pass this law by *popular vote* and the campaign was led by drag queen Panti Bliss, who has become known as The Queen of Ireland.

Did you know?
- *RuPaul's Drag Race* has won multiple Emmy Awards – a lot of popular slang words that originate in the trans and queer community, make their way into the general public through shows like this. Slayyyy!
- Most pirates had gay relationships! They'd spend so long at sea that they'd seek comfort in each other.
- Madonna did not invent the dance 'Vogue'. It was established as part of the drag Ball Culture in 1970s New York.
- Ball Culture began in the 1920s when drag fashion shows were performed by mostly white men. It was not a welcoming or safe space for Black and Latinx members of the community. As a result, they created their own Ballroom Scene where they could express themselves freely and securely.

- Chosen families blossomed from the community of the Ballroom Scene, with houses of 'drag mothers' and 'drag daughters' educating and supporting one another.

♡ Being LGBTQIA+ is part of nature

Same-gender pairing is so common in the animal kingdom that there are more than 1,000 species documented as practising same-gender coupling. In fact, homosexual behaviour in animals has been observed for more than 2,000 years. A few examples? Male giraffes have been known to engage in homosexual behaviour and so have both male and female lions. Male elephants often live apart from the herd so they can engage sexually with other males. Both male and female bottlenose dolphins engage in homosexual practice. Bonobos, those adorable chimpanzees, are bisexual, and wild bison are known to frequently engage in male-to-male sexual activities. Albatrosses stay with their same-gender partners for life, and a whopping 25 per cent of black swans are gay. Male walruses are homosexual before they mature – the list goes on and on, but we will end with our favourite. **Male gay penguins have been known to adopt abandoned eggs, making a family of their own!**

♡ Straight up

The love, support and advocacy of our allies is so important, so the last word on Pride goes to our dear friend, supermum Felicity of @harfinfamily.

So Felicity – what does 'Pride' and being an ally mean to you?

Pride is a celebration. A needed one still. We deserve to celebrate, at the same time as learning about different people and different types of love. I've grown up being an ally, and it's important to me to celebrate my friends and stand with a community that was previously so alone.

Rainbow Stories: Pride

Members of the Community share what living with Pride means to them.

Kathy, 21

Living with Pride, for me, means being my most unabashedly queer self. It means fully accepting that I am who I am – and realising that no self-repression or outside force is going to change that. I am gloriously comfortable in my queerness on behalf of the younger version of me who never believed she would be.

Paula, 23

Living with Pride kind of means rebellion. It means living as myself with whoever I want *defiantly*, no matter what stupid thing certain ignorant people have to say about it. I will never be able to understand how people can have negative views about someone based on anything as superficial as their sexuality. Everyone is a human. All that people should need to be for others' acceptance is a good human being.

How I see it, everyone is a good human until they prove you wrong. And that's also how I'd like others to view their fellow man; assume people are good until they give you reason not to think they're good.

Boo, 19

I don't think I live with Pride per se, but I don't live with shame. I just live as me, and it's not a big thing. That's the reason why I'm not as big into Pride as most people. I think it's because, for me, I don't feel like I *need* it. But I also understand that for others it makes them feel a sense of community and acceptance. I'm lucky in that I don't need to seek it out, I have thankfully always had a loving, non-judgemental support system around me; but I hope that those who need Pride find the family they deserve.

Chris, 21

Living with Pride is a pretty loaded statement. It's hard to say how much of that I do and how much is just existing, really; but I guess, to exist the way we do is to exist in constant rebellion, and one can only rebel in favour of that which they would never wish to change. Maybe that's it. Maybe throughout all of the self-discovery, changing labels, changing pronouns, changing them back, then into something new, then nothing, then everything, then finding it, finding me in cool, new words, there is me who may not always know who they are but knows that they should be. I should have been allowed to know who I was as a child, rather than being shielded from it. I should have been allowed to come out as a teenager and not be met with bullying at school and at home. I should have been allowed to change my label, change my pronouns, change my mind and then do it again in my formative years without being chastised by both my community and the people standing outside it with pitchforks. I should be whatever way I am, and I should be accepted for it – just as I accept myself.

Sam, 26

Pride as a riot, Pride as violence and finally, Pride as a display of beauty and new-age tolerance. As the world has changed, so has Pride as an event and as a lifestyle. Naturally, the celebration of Pride Month has become a huge spectacle and is by far the most colourful day in Dublin's calendar. The real search for Pride must be internal – because it is in those breathless moments when you are running from a group of men on a dimly lit street that you have to find the proud spirit inside you to continue. That's where my greatest struggle with Pride has always been. Most of my friends are LGBTQIA+ at this age, and sometimes, living in the echo chamber, I forget about what's going on outside it. The moments when you leave a bar and are making your way home and suddenly realise you are at risk. While they are terrifying, they are the ultimate display of Pride. It's in situations like these that the rhythmic drumming on the Pride parade needs to take hold of your chest and remind you who you really are.

Matthew and Ryan chat with...

Jamie Raines (@jammi.dodger), **a fellow content creator and LGBT advocate**, about all things LGBTQIA+ and his recent wedding!

M&R: When did you first think you were a part of our community?

Jamie: My first realisation that I was LGBTQIA+ in some way was when I was a teenager (before I realised I was trans, and so I was living as a girl at the time), and I was like, oh wow, I think I like girls and boys – am I bi?! I then briefly identified as a lesbian, until I realised I was trans by total accident after I watched a documentary about a trans guy. This documentary gave me the language to describe something I'd felt about myself for as long as I could remember.

M&R: Can you tell us a bit about how the whole 'coming-out' experience was for you?

Jamie: I had several coming outs; I feel as if I was in some kind of layered closet! When I came out as bi/lesbian before realising I was trans, I didn't find that too difficult. I knew my closest friends and family would likely be supportive – and they were – because they were all accepting of other people who were LGB. Coming out as trans was much scarier; I was less sure about people's reactions. I ended up having a huge amount of support that I'm so grateful for but definitely lost more friends and heard more negative whispering going around about me than when I'd come out in terms of my sexuality. I'm not saying one is objectively harder than another; this is just what happened to me.

Something I took away from it is that coming out can show you who your true friends and supporters are, and there is always support out there – even if it's not always in the most obvious places.

M&R: Did you experience much confusion so far along the journey?

Jamie: I've had a lot of confusion over the years about my sexuality, especially before I realised I was trans. The way I was feeling just didn't make sense to me, identifying as a lesbian didn't feel right to me. I did this because everyone assumed I was because of the way I looked and behaved. There was no confusion around being trans for me though, and over time my sexuality made more sense to me too.

M&R: Do you have a preferred definition of your sexuality?

Jamie: Bisexual – and it's been a *journey*. I just never had the same sure feeling of knowing my sexuality that I had over knowing my gender. When I was younger, I was desperate to find a label for it that felt perfect, but over the years I've kind of just accepted that I like who I like, and bisexual feels like the best fit for who I like.

M&R: What are your pronouns, and what was your experience of discovering them like?

Jamie: My pronouns are he/him, and my journey was pretty much realising that I'm trans and that I could live as the boy I'd always felt I was, and that was that.

M&R: How do you deal with bullies?

Jamie: They're not worth your time, honestly. Especially online bullies, I just block them, mute them, ignore them. They're just out there spreading negativity for no reason, and they probably go around saying bad things to lots of people. There's nothing wrong with me, I'm not the problem, they clearly have an issue with certain people and feel the need to share that. So, I just focus on the supportive people, the lovely kind comments, the heart-warming stories, my friends and family, and I don't let the bullies take the positive moments away from me.

M&R: Have you experienced any mental health issues throughout your journey?

Jamie: Not anything specific to my journey, but regardless of why someone might experience mental health issues, it's always okay to tell someone and ask for help, and it's not a sign of weakness.

M&R: What does living with pride mean for you?

Jamie: Pride means not just surviving but thriving as an LGBT+ person. I know who I am, I have amazing friends and family around me, and no hate or bigotry can take that away from me. I'm proud of who I am, proud of my journey and proud of my achievements. Reaching this point and feeling that I'm living with pride, and have pride in who I am, has been incredibly freeing.

M&R: You have spoken about anxiety online. Do you have any advice for younger people dealing with similar issues?

Jamie: Honestly, talk to people about it. I bottled it up and hid away so much of my anxiety for YEARS, and only now am I actually talking about it fully openly with people and also digging into the root of it.

I know it's super hard to talk about certain things, and to certain people, but you don't have to battle it on your own. You're not alone in the way you're feeling, and there is support and advice out there that can really help.

M&R: Would you be comfortable giving us a brief outline of the process of transitioning, for young people out there who need a first-hand resource?

Jamie: Transitioning is multi-layered, personal, and there's no right or wrong way to go about it. Typically, you can split transitioning into social and medical elements. Social is the aspects of coming out, living and presenting as your true gender – this could include changing your pronouns, your name, changing your hair and what clothes you wear. Then the medical side includes things like puberty blockers, hormones such as testosterone and oestrogen, and surgeries.

But just know, you don't have to pursue any stages that aren't right for you. No one transition journey is the same. Not everyone changes their name or gets a haircut; there's no requirement to take hormones, and many trans people do not want or need any surgeries. You are allowed to transition in the way that works for *you.*

When you're first realising you're trans, I would advise you to take some time for yourself and work through your feelings. Then I would tell one person, or a small number of close and/or trusted people who you are confident will be there for you and accept you. Having just one person who accepts and supports you can really help going forward. At this point, I would start considering how you might want to proceed, whether that's coming out slowly to more and more people, a big announcement, letting everyone know about a change of name and/or pronouns and so on.

Take things a little bit at a time, go at your own pace, and remember that there's no wrong way to do this.

In terms of logistically how to actually transition, the legal and healthcare processes differ depending on where you live. For example, in the UK we have the NHS that offers treatment to transgender people, and the first step would be to talk to your doctor to get referred to a gender clinic. It's the gender clinic that will be able to diagnose you, offer specialist support and counselling, recommend things like hormones, and refer you for surgery. But obviously this isn't a universal pattern. A good way to start to find out how the process works where you live is having a look online, seeing if there are any local charities or support groups that can advise you, and talking to anyone you know who may also be trans living in the area.

M&R: For parents out there who may be feeling nervous about the process of transitioning, do you have any words of comfort to offer?

Jamie: Your child is still the same child they were before they came out/started transitioning, and allowing them to be themselves is the best thing you can do for them.

Support is the most important thing for trans people, especially trans kids, and they deserve to be allowed to be themselves and to be supported, loved and accepted for who they are.

Saying that, it's okay if you're taken aback, shocked or need some time to process – it's pretty big news! Just do your best to use new pronouns and names, and listen to how your child is feeling and what they need to do. Maybe even try going to some joint counselling sessions if you're really struggling; that way you can share your feelings, and listen to your child's feelings, in a safe environment where someone else can guide you both through this process and the changes it has brought.**M&R: Your wedding to Shaaba looked like a real celebration of joy! What do you think**

marriage means for our community, and how did it feel to celebrate?

Jamie: I think marriage and weddings are an industry that's massively cis-heteronormative still. Gay marriage has been legal for less than a decade in the UK, and trans people require a gender recognition certificate to get married as their correct gender (and they're difficult and invasive to get – only around 2% of trans people in the UK have one). Because there are these hurdles to overcome, and negative judgements from others, it can almost feel like an even bigger celebration. Being able to legally show love and commitment to one another, as well as share that with your family and friends, is very special.

Shaaba and I had a pretty difficult journey with acceptance of our relationship from some family members, and the moment of being able to stand in front of everyone, including those who have come on a massive journey from unacceptance to acceptance, felt amazing. We wanted to make sure that all the faces we would look out and see during our wedding ceremony would be of people who genuinely supported us and were there to celebrate with us, and they were.

The happiest parts of the day included the first time I saw Shaaba walking down the aisle. We went a little traditional here and hadn't seen each other since the evening before. A wedding is a day of high nerves, and all either of us wanted was to be back together, so finally seeing each other – there were a lot of emotions! Then the ceremony itself was very special; we had an amazing celebrant who did a beautiful job of telling our story, and it was just personal to us.

CHAPTER 5
Mental Health

Having good mental health is important for everyone. And for those of us who are part of the Rainbow Community, it is especially important that we don't just look after each other but that we look after ourselves. We all get down sometimes; that's unfortunately a part of the human experience, and it's normal!

♡ What is mental health?

Mental health is our overall sense of well-being and how we feel we are getting on in our lives, as well as how we feel about ourselves and those around us.

Broadly speaking, having good mental health means you are able to do the basic things in life with relative ease and happiness, such as:

- have a reasonably positive attitude
- get on okay with other people
- feel able to do your work or studies
- cope with normal demands of life

- feel comfortable in your own skin
- make a contribution to the world around you.

When our mental health is good, we can enjoy life and feel good about ourselves. It means we are capable of dealing with problems and tough times in our lives when they come along.

The reason why it's important for us to cover mental health in this book is because experiences like homophobia and transphobia can lead to additional stress for LGBTQIA+ people, which can have a negative impact on their mental health, sometimes leading to serious problems such as anxiety or depression.

There is *lots* of support available from helplines, LGBTQIA+ organisations and mainstream support services.

If you have *any* concerns about your own mental health, or that of your loved ones, you'll find contact numbers in our Resources section at the end of this book.

Mental health is especially important to all of us in the Rainbow Community because the experience of being ourselves in a world that identifies us as different can cause a particular type of hurt.

MATTHEW

'I was afraid to be myself.'

When I was about 13, I was asked out by a girl, and, although I didn't fancy her one tiny bit, I felt like I had to say yes to going out with her to stop people asking me if I was gay. People then asked both of us if I was gay or asked her if she knew that she was dating a gay person! I absolutely knew that I was not attracted to her whatsoever, but it was more of a childhood cover-up to try and hide who I really was. I was unintentionally using her to hide my true self.

She must have picked up on how I was feeling, because she dumped me after just six weeks for another boy, and I felt so relieved because it was a mess I didn't need to worry about any more. I pretty much spent the whole summer studying by myself and wondering what an earth my life was. I don't even think I was happy or sad, I just quite simply felt 'meh'. Looking back, I think I was in a sort of depression – or at least, not connected with my life.

We both feel sad when we think of some of the things we went through in the past, but it has led us to being even more grateful and connected to the life we have today. Enjoying the small things in life and staying upbeat is a work in progress. Our life isn't perfect, but we try and do as much as we can to keep a positive attitude and lead a healthy life – inside and out.

Here are some of the most useful ways we have found to help us stay mentally on top.

1. Going offline

Put down the phone and take a step back. As content creators we can be very easily consumed by social media, always looking at others and comparing what they're doing and achieving. So taking a step back and doing something offline is really important for us. We do a lot of gardening. We love it as we can enjoy the peace of it and love being surrounded by nature, together. We also like going on hikes, adventuring to new places and simply just playing with our dog. We struggle with switching off, so when we finally do it, we love it! We've learned that it's important to slow down without making ourselves feel guilty. We believe that everyone needs time to recharge, whether that's with a hearty meal or a good bubble bath.

2. Creativity feeds the soul

Making things is so relaxing. Creativity, using our hands to make something – whether it's playing video games or making a pot – really helps us to switch off. Ryan escapes into his make-up and can easily get lost playing with products and creating looks. Matthew loves pottery and gets out of his head and stuck into the pottery wheel! Creating things is something we love doing individually and together.

3. Healthy body, healthy mind

Gym and exercise are important in keeping stress at bay. It sounds a cliché but going to the gym or going for a long walk with our dog Roscoe really helps to reduce our anxieties and makes us feel better when we're overwhelmed with life. There's a huge release of endorphins involved!

We usually workout early, and we have to encourage ourselves to go as we find it *a lot* easier to stay in bed. However, because there's two of us, it's easy for one of us to force the other; who is feeling lazier changes by the day.

Of course, we still think of our anxieties and problems while we are at the gym or running, but somehow they seem smaller after we've done some exercise. We lead busy lives, so there are some weeks where we can't stick to our workout plans because we are away or swamped with work. This used to make us feel bad about ourselves, but we've got to a place now where we are a bit more chilled and realise that we can't do everything! Forgiving ourselves for not being perfect is important too!

> *Georgina Watson,*
> *Ryan's childhood friend*
> 'Ryan is a ray of sunshine. My mum has always said that with Ryan comes laughter!'

4. Sweets and sustenance

A good diet means chocolate too! Food is a big one for us. We're in a place now where we simply enjoy food, and it's sometimes a reward for us. So if we've had a tough day or week, we feel it justifies us eating something 'bad'. Generally though, we do try to eat cleanly and have a balanced diet as we feel it helps with our energy levels and how we feel about ourselves – and if we eat badly, the next day the gym is just a little bit harder! However, we do believe that treating ourselves is important too; that's part of the balance.

Of the two of us, Matthew has the biggest sweet tooth and will often slip a small chocolate snack throughout the day. Eating the food which gives us a serotonin boost is something that we feel is very beneficial when we're down.

A mixture of comfort foods and healthy foods makes us feel better when our mental health is bad. For example, a snack or treat is something that makes us feel better in the short term, and after eating a healthy meal we automatically feel a bit better about ourselves because we know we've given our body something good and nutritious. We also enjoy going for dinner or cooking together as it's time we get to spend with one another and bond.

'Optimism is my best trait. I've grown up to be such a positive and optimistic person, and, to be honest with you, I feel like this is one of my biggest and best traits; even in the worst situations I can bring out the positive. I think it's because I've always known that no matter who I surround myself with or what situation I'm in, there's a huge, wide world out there, and whatever is happening isn't the be all and end all.'
Matthew

5. Communication is KEY

A problem shared is a problem halved. It's wonderful being in a relationship in which we both value open communication. Ryan has always been a very open person who wears his heart on his sleeve. For him, it's essential to be able to express your emotions honestly and openly. Similarly, Matthew is a very outgoing person and loves talking to people. Being honest and open with people is something that comes really naturally to him, and people gravitate towards his good energy.

We're open with our online family because we really enjoy communicating with them, and we find it mind-blowing that we can communicate with people all across the world. We pride ourselves on being authentic, and this goes hand in hand with good communication. We go live quite a lot on social media where we'll have chats and deep conversations while cooking dinner together or simply talking.

If we're having a bad day, we explain that it's okay, and being honest with our audience encourages them to give back, so we learn a lot from them too.

When it comes to communicating with each other over difficult stuff, it's easier said than done. But, because we're together all the time, we like to hash things out immediately if we feel as if there's something wrong. Saying it straight away helps squash any negativity quickly. It definitely works for us; communication really is key.

6. Friendships are important

Find people who share the same experiences and stories. We have a lot of mutual friends, but, of course, we do talk to them individually as well. It's quite nice to be able to talk to someone about any issues that we have or just to vent about our feelings without the other person being there.

It's really important to open up to friends and talk to the people around you. It's helpful to get a different perspective on whatever we're going through. Other people often see things in a different light, which can be more positive than what our negative mental health makes us feel or believe at the time.

Our family and friends understand how hard-working and passionate we are in what we do. It's also quite nice to have some friends who are in the online content-creating industry; we talk about things that aren't related to social media, but we can also help each other with the creative process because we can get and give a new perspective from a fresh set of eyes.

Another thing we love to do is play board games with friends and families. It's really fun to get together with people, chat, laugh and play a game or two. It's a great way to bond, chat and have a bit of competitive fun over who'll win. We love that we can do these things with friends and family because it's these sorts of things that you look back on and smile about when you think of your fond memories with other people.

Expressing loooooveee

Make each other feel special. We enjoy having a good date night, either ordering a pizza or getting loads of yummy snacks and watching a good Netflix film at home on the sofa in our PJs. As much as we love venturing around and exploring new places and new opportunities, we also love to just put on a film and relax. Winding down and doing nothing is sometimes the nicest thing we can do together.

Ryan: A memory that I will always cherish is my 21st birthday. We had only been together around four or five months before

I turned 21. I remember that Matthew was so thoughtful and caring and really showed his giving side. He got me the best cake I've ever seen, and no one in my life has ever treated me the way he treated me. It wasn't even about what he got me; it was the fact that he made time after work to see me and wanted to do whatever I wanted. He gave me his attention wholeheartedly the entire day and wasn't distracted, or on his phone or messaging anyone else, and I found it very, very sweet.

Another really important memory I have of Matthew is when my mum passed away. He was really there for me. Even though Matthew likes to make situations lighthearted, during this time he showed me just how sensitive and caring he could be. He was there for me at the funeral, never leaving my side and constantly checking in and making sure that I was okay. This showed me a whole new side to Matthew, and made me love him more.

Matthew: A memory that sticks out for me is when I had a birthday during lockdown. Ryan made sure that I had a really good birthday despite everything. He set up a really special Pokémon-themed party for me at home. He decorated the house and bought all of my favourite foods and snacks and made sure my day was really special, even though it was just us. It's easy to get a pass card when things like lockdown happen, but the fact that Ryan went out of his way to make my birthday a special day was really sweet.

8. Laughter

Having a laugh is literal happiness! Although we do a lot of pranks online, we have quite a jokey relationship off-line too. We love playing jokes on each other and having laughs. Sometimes we just need to remind each other to have this type of fun and to live in the moment.

For fun, we love exploring and seeing new places. For us, having new memories and creating really great content to look back on is what we call fun. We started creating content for fun back in 2015/2016 and it's always stayed like that. We've made sure that, even though creating content has become our jobs, it remains fun for us – so that we can sustain it and keep doing it forever! We always try to have fun by enjoying whatever we're filming and try to make positive memories through whatever we're doing, so we can look back when we're old and know that we had a good time.

9. Baby Roscoe

It's a fact that pets are good for your mental health. It's very hard to explain how you can simply just look at your animal and feel their love for you, and how it just gives you a calming energy. They help you see love and positivity in the world because they love you so much.

We think getting Roscoe also pushed us to go outside more often. We love going on long walks with him. It's also quite nice because Matthew's family is always close and they all have dogs, so it's good that all the family dogs get along and they get to play together often.

We think it's really rewarding and fulfilling to care for another being.

Here's a top tip from LGBT+ young people's charity Just Like Us on how to deal with feeling lonely

Lots of people feel lonely when they first realise they're LGBT+. Finding community and getting to know other LGBT+ people often helps us feel safer, happier and more connected. Not sure where to go? Switchboard is a LGBT+ charity that has a really helpful online chat where they can signpost you to things in your local area.

Top ten tips for mental health

1. **Put down your phone:** Switch off, get out and take time to experience the world.
2. **Keep in touch:** Look after friends and family, and they will look after you.
3. **Stay active:** Take regular exercise – try and get out for a walk every day.
4. **Talk:** Openly communicate your thoughts and feelings to make them less scary and easier to manage.
5. **Appeal to your senses:** Listen to the birds. Smell the freshly baked bread. Feel the sun on your skin. Stay in touch with your senses to stay centred.
6. **Make leisure a priority:** Take time off from work and study to get out there and have fun.
7. **Eat balanced meals:** We're not experts, but we have read that foods that can support your

mood include fatty fish, rich in omega-3s; nuts; avocados; beans; leafy greens; fresh fruit and, yes, CHOCOLATE (but not too much!)!
8. **Don't skimp on sleep:** Sleep is our body and mind's way to recharge. Take a break from all screens for an hour before bedtime. Read a book or listen to a podcast instead.
9. **Seek help from a professional:** There is no shame in needing help – that's what therapists are there for! There are lots counsellors who specialise in LGBTQIA+ issues, and you can find information about finding one from the websites in our Resources section.
10. **Find purpose and meaning:** Be creative. Take on a hobby you love. Help other people. Think about what you were put on this earth to do, and try to do it!

LOVE IS LOVE MOMENT:
Proud dad

He's my son, and I am so proud of all he's achieved. All that hard work. He amazes me. I had tears in my eyes at his graduation.

Ryan's dad

CHAPTER 6
How to Beat the Bullies!
(Not Physically, Obvs...)

Bullies have always been there, and it is their mission to pick on people and make their lives a misery; it makes them feel bigger and more important than they are. This is because bullies – by their very nature – are insecure people with low self-esteem! Often, bullies are secretly self-conscious, and they bully others to gain a feeling of purpose and control in their lives. Sometimes, bullies themselves are the victims of bullying by others (or they were in the past), so they repeat the same behaviour to try to regain their power. Of course, this does NOT make it okay.

MATTHEW

'I got teased in school.'

Because I had flamboyant mannerisms, people began asking me if I was gay as soon as I started secondary school. I was often teased for talking a certain way, walking a certain way or carrying myself a certain way. It didn't help that all my friends were girls, and I would never hang around with boys. Secondary school was full of lots of people who wanted to show off in front of their friends, and I always just felt so closed off from boys because of the fear of being rejected for being gay.

During school, pranks were a big thing. I heard that a group of nasty girls had called my mum one evening and told her that I was gay. Apparently this happened when I was 15, but I wasn't told about it until I was leaving school at 16. It really showed me how cruel some people can be. My mum never mentioned it to me, and she was so right not to tell me because if I had known about it when it happened, it would have been even more stressful. Even though it was dreadful, I feel lucky that I have a mum who was really looking out for me.

♡ Online bullies

Online bullies can be a real problem because the internet gives people the anonymity and the ability to say hateful things without being face to face. We try to keep our hearts and minds open, and we also believe that most nasty behaviour is caused by ignorance – either because the person has no experience of LGBTQIA+ people in their lives or has maybe lived in a culture or a community that is homophobic, as many fundamentalist religions still are.

As Matthew and Ryan, we put our lives online because we believe in standing up and being purposefully visible as a gay couple. We both knew that there would be haters, and it took a lot of unhealthy scrolling through the hate before we learned to mute the cruel critics and fully focus on the outpouring of love from our true fans.

♡ School bullies still exist

Bullying from your peers, the people you want to fit in and be friends with, is possibly the most painful part of growing up LGBTQIA+. While people, especially young people, are definitely more accepting than they were even when we were in school, we are shocked at the number of stories that still come through to us from our followers who are being bullied at school and online. At school, we both experienced bullying, so we know how painful and confusing it can be. It is so easy to blame yourself and feel as if there is something wrong with *you* because you are being picked on. But this is absolutely not true. So if you are the victim of bullying, remember it is all about the bully being a bully and nothing to do with fabulous you.

To help you out, here are our top ways of dealing with bullying:

1. Talk to someone. Don't suffer in silence.
2. Know that you are not alone.
3. Block or report any bullying or abuse.
4. Ignore the hate and surround yourself with love.
5. Always stay safe.

1. Talk to someone. Don't suffer in silence.

Our most important tip when dealing with bullying is to talk to someone. You might feel as if you are on your own, but often your friends and family might be more open to talking than you think. Sometimes it is our own fears holding us back from sharing with our loved ones, so take a deep breath and try. However, some of us do not have that close network of people we can turn to, and sometimes that's why the bullies cruelly pick them out. The good news is that bullying is recognised for the toxic thing it is – by EVERYONE! So, it's important for you to know that the teachers, staff and counsellors at your school have a professional duty to deal with this issue. It's part of their job, so don't be afraid to talk with them. You might get a different perspective on the situation from them, which might be helpful too. It's essential not to suffer in silence because otherwise the bullying might not stop, and you need people around you to advise and protect you.

Sometimes people think that being bullied is shameful, so they don't speak up, but that's exactly what the bullies want. Don't isolate yourself – reach out to someone you feel you can trust.

Some of us don't feel comfortable talking to anyone in person, and that's when going online, or reaching out on social media, can be very helpful. A lot of the time, it can be easier to go and speak to someone online to ask for help, such as an online charity or a forum group. There's a ton of online community groups out there to talk to, so if you feel as if you can't talk to your family or you don't want to talk to a teacher then you can talk to someone online in confidence and know that you've been heard and get some advice. Check out more details in our Resources section.

It takes a lot of courage and effort to go and speak to someone and ask for help. Remember, your family and friends love you, and they're always going to have your best interests at heart; that's why they are there.

2. Know that you are not alone

We can't stress this enough; when you're being bullied, you might feel as if you're alone and that no one around you is there to help or that they won't be able to do anything about it. This isn't the case at all. It's really important to remember that there are lots of people in this world who care for you who'll be able to help when they realise you're being bullied. It's also important to stress that if you are being bullied it isn't a sign of weakness or there being something wrong with you; it's the bully who is wrong.

3. Block or report any bullying or abuse

If you're being bullied or you receive hate online, it's really important to make sure that you report it on whatever social media it comes from. You can screenshot any messages, group chats, calls or things like that for proof of harassment should you need it, but the most important thing is to report it. There are procedures in place on all social media sites where they can review it and safeguard your well-being. By blocking someone who's bullying you, it allows you to simply take yourself out of the situation and put a wall between you and the online bully. Blocking someone can be quite difficult as sometimes you might fear that you're running away – but you're actually taking charge of the situation! You've taken control and decided enough is enough by blocking the bully, completely defusing their attacks. It also sends a message to the person that you will not entertain it or allow this to happen.

It's sometimes really tempting to comment back, but that's exactly what they want. They are looking for a reaction, and, by blocking them and not giving them the satisfaction of a response, it shows that you will not play their games.

4. Ignore the hate and surround yourself with love

When you are being bullied, it's really easy to think that you're at fault or that there's something wrong with you, when in fact you've done nothing wrong, and, unfortunately, you are just a victim. It's really important to know that you are loved. The best way forward is to surround yourself with the people who make you feel loved and to do the things that make you happy and that make you LAUGH! For example, you could go for a bike ride, watch a movie, go out for ice cream – do something with your friends and family. By surrounding yourself with people you love and who love you, you will be entering your happy place, making you feel safe and cocooned from the hatred of ignorant bullies.

Ignore them as best you can because they'll likely get bored and stop when they're not getting the attention they hoped for.

5. Always stay safe

It's very important that you don't put yourself in any situation where you might end up getting hurt! It's never a good idea to meet bullies on your own. Sometimes people have really negative intentions, and it's good to try and stay out of it as much as possible and not get involved physically.

There's a range of ways you can stay safe, such as simply not interacting with the bully, but the safest bet is to tell your family and friends or someone that you know who can help you, such as a teacher, online group or even the police if things get too serious. Safety is the most important thing in the world, and, even though sometimes we're tempted to stand our ground, it's pointless to put yourself at risk of harm as there are far more effective ways to handle the situation, not to mention ways that are far more scary for the bully.

We called in the experts at the LGBT+ young people's charity Just Like Us to give us their best advice:

How to deal with bullying (in school and online)

1. If you're being bullied or made to feel unsafe, it's really important to tell a trusted adult. Maybe there is a teacher that's approachable at school? All schools have a duty to stop bullying, keep all pupils safe and make sure anti-LGBT+ language isn't being used in school. Or maybe there is someone at home or at a youth group/club you could tell? If it's making you feel uncomfortable, it's not okay. Speak to an adult so they can help – even if you're not sure if it counts as bullying.
2. If someone is treating you or your friends unkindly online, you can block them and report it to stop it. Make sure you tell someone too.

3. Get support from Childline or Switchboard, an LGBT+ charity with an online chat and phone helpline with kind volunteers ready to listen.
4. If you're worried about a friend, check in on them and ask how they're doing. If they are facing bullying or feel uncomfortable with something that's happening, it's really important to tell an adult.

True Life Story: Rain Preece (he/they)

'Coming out was a really positive experience. The best bit was choosing my new name.'

My name is Rain. I picked it out myself. I wanted a name that wasn't particularly tied down to male or female. This is because I am transgender, meaning my gender isn't the same as the one that was assigned to me at birth. I wanted a name that would help me feel freer from gendered expectations.

I discovered what being trans was by seeing a documentary, and my first thought was *Could that be me?* and it really frightened me but also in a beautiful way made me think more clearly about what other people assumed were body image issues and low self-esteem. I went through a tough time trying to find out who I was. My mental health was very up and down.

I also got diagnosed with autism when I was 15. There are some negative assumptions out there that being autistic means that you're less able to know yourself when it comes to gender identity. This isn't true at all, and there are actually lots of trans autistic people. We're no less able to determine our gender identity than anyone else.

For me, coming out was a really positive experience. The best bit was choosing my new name. I looked up what gender-neutral names were out there and made a shortlist. I then called a family meeting to get my family on board with deciding what my name would be. It was really nice getting the family involved because I felt that this milestone helped them understand me better.

As a trans person, I have faced many challenges in everyday life and still do. At school, I was ridiculed, laughed at and pushed against a sink, just for trying to use a bathroom. I wish I'd had more LGBT+ inclusive education and support at school and an LGBT+ role model to speak to.

Thankfully, I now volunteer with Just Like Us, the LGBT+ young people's charity, to make schools a better place for trans young people. I volunteer with the charity to speak in secondary schools about what it's like to be trans and how pupils can be better allies. I can now be the visible trans representation that I wish I'd had growing up.

My main message for anyone out there who is questioning their sexuality or gender is to know that it is okay to question and that you are not alone. If you think you might be trans, I want you to know that there will always be people out there who want to support you and love you for who you are – sometimes it just takes time to find them. Lastly, for trans autistic people, please know that you are wonderful beings, who are so valid and deserve to be believed and encouraged to be who you really are.

CHAPTER 7
For the Parents

Our parents are the most important people in our lives, and how they respond to us being LGBTQIA+ can have a huge impact on our lives. As we said in the Coming Out chapter, sometimes having a child who comes to you to talk about their gender and sexual orientation is no big deal, but other times it can come as a surprise, and in some cultures and circumstances, a shock.

Sometimes parents need time to educate themselves and gather the information they need to adjust to this news. This chapter is specifically for the parents. We have gathered advice from our own parents, as well as pyschotherapist Joanna Fortune, and our dear friend and supermum, Felicity Harfin, to give parents – and you – the information and advice they might need.

All parents just want to do the right thing for their children. However, it's not always clear what the right thing is, and sometimes the 'right' thing might turn out to be the wrong thing. The most important thing to remember is that no matter how your parents might react at first, when love is behind everyone's motives things will always turn out okay.

MATTHEW

'Mum told me that she always knew.'

I was so nervous on the lead-up to coming out to my mum. As I texted her asking her to come up to my bedroom, my heart was pounding, but even just hearing her footsteps coming up the stairs, I had a strange burst of relief beginning to come over me. The conversation lasted around 30 seconds. We've never really spoken about it since, but it was just instantly accepted. I don't really know what else I expected. Her reaction was accepting but calm. To be honest, I felt slightly underwhelmed after all the build-up but also really relieved. It quite simply wasn't a big deal at all. I also felt so grateful that I didn't have to deal with a huge, negative coming-out family experience.

My son Matthew: Allison Mackinnon

Matthew's Mum, Allison, is like a mum to both of us. She is the epitome of love is love. She's a mum and we are her boys. She never judges or makes us feel different from any other couple.

I couldn't ask for better

Matthew and I have always had a very close relationship. I couldn't ask for better, I'm very proud of him.

Our favourite time together for years was watching *Buffy*. His sister is four years older than him, so she'd be out doing her own thing, and his dad would be out watching the football. Our duvets would be brought down to the living room.

We went through God knows how many series – he has all the DVDs, and he's even collected the figures. I had to go to some way-out, weird shop in London to get them for him! I didn't mind because it was really wonderful. For any teenager to still want to sit with his mum and watch TV is a gift.

Will they find love?

With conversations around coming out, initially there's a little bit of worry. You want them to be safe, and you want them to be happy. No one wants to think of their child being picked on or facing prejudice. The big question is – will they find love? You just have to be open with each other. I know that's easier said than done in some families, but prioritise having an openness in the relationship if you can.

Seeking support

Forming a close circle really makes a lot of difference. Matthew was shy early on, but he always made lots of friends. Sometimes I can't believe the things he does now, like public speaking and presenting awards. Over time, his confidence has grown into something beautiful.

He always had a great network of friends in school who he trusted. A lot of them became friends for life. That support system was so important for Matthew as these were the first people he welcomed in. They were so supportive of him and helped him through a lot to become the person he is today.

Old school books full of kind notes from teachers and friends are a testament to him growing up. Matthew was bubbly and bright, and everyone adored him for it. One night in school they had an awards night. Matthew was voted most likely to be on the cover of *Hello* magazine! He's always been a kind, friendly person.

What if I say the wrong thing?

For a parent, a conversation around coming out can seem quite overwhelming. It's hard to know the right thing to say in the moment.

It's important to act as normal as possible. It's a huge thing for a young person to say those words to their mum or dad, just like it was for Matthew. I acted really cool and didn't make a big deal of it. I didn't want to appear shocked.

Treat it as if it is the most normal thing in the world – because it is!

Your feelings never change for them.

My only apprehension was the older generations of our family. Back in their day it wasn't as common to be open about sexuality. There was a concern that there might be a shift in how they treated him – but nothing changed. We met Matthew with love and acceptance.

It's heartbreaking for some children to have a negative reaction. Ryan didn't have a particularly good experience. You can see both sides of what happens. I'm incredibly proud of Ryan. He's turned it all around now. It's amazing!

In Matthew's youth, there wasn't as much awareness. There's much more guidance now for young people. Conversations have opened up everywhere. Social media has had a massive impact on everyone's lives. There is a lot of input from their followers on TikTok and their other social media platforms who say they've inspired them to come out to their own friends and family. Even through the internet they share pride.

Pride is all around us

When you see a family out and it's two dads, it fills you with pride. In my generation, there wasn't an option to live so openly. It's fantastic, and I look forward to it when the time is right for them. They've got a lot of travelling to do first!

I have to say I'm most proud of Matthew's drive to better himself. Since school he's always done well for himself despite how he struggled. He had a good retail job and then became a manager of Boots opticians. The decision to go to university came at a later date. We were all overcome by his ambition! That's what I'm most proud of him for.

Family members will always say Matthew is such a thoughtful person. My mum in particular has a soft spot for him. Since his grandad passed away seven years ago, he's always been right there for her. It makes me so proud to see him looking out for her.

The view Matthew has on the world is totally glass half full. He's kind, ambitious, thoughtful and positive. I couldn't have asked for a better son.

Where we are now...

Gardening is our passion. We go to garden centres with his nan, have coffee and a cake. Sometimes we'll go with Ryan and have lunch. Those boys love their roses. It's a very grown-up thing to do now – and we always come home with a new plant!

The garden shows are amazing as well. We're really enjoying that at the moment. Yeah, I know it sounds boring, but we're normal! The boys are taking me shopping on Friday. We're going to have a proper catch up on what they've been doing – because I can't keep up with them!

We're still very close. He only lives down the road! At some point they may move away, and I don't know how I feel about that. I'll miss them not being ten minutes away.

My son Ryan: Malcom Payne

Malcom Payne is Ryan's dad, and they have always been close. Here, Malcolm talks about what Ryan was like as a child, their relationship, the painful mistake he made around his son coming out and how they have come through it all, happier and closer than ever.

Ryan was such a chirpy, well-mannered little boy. Back when he used to go to nursery and playschool he was always fun and always enjoyed going to the parks. When we used to kick the football around a bit, he didn't enjoy it much – I think he was doing it for me. That's the kind of lad he was.

In his youth he was very shy. School was a struggle for him early on. I knew that because I was often in and out of the school, being told he was falling behind in his classes. Bullies were out to get him, so he had little interest in school. It was a struggle even to get him to do his homework, so what he achieved in getting his master's degree is beyond me. I'm incredibly proud.

He always liked to help his nan when she was struggling. She would take him swimming, then he'd go down to her for dinner. Ryan wouldn't have a bad name said against her. I suppose he looked at my mum as a nan *and* a mum, seeing as he didn't have his own.

'Whatever Ryan turns out to be, just support him'

Ryan was still very young when his nan said something one day that stuck with me: *'Whatever Ryan turns out to be, just support him.'* He used to go to his nan's and talk to her; he wouldn't come to me. What she was alluding to didn't register with me at the time, but when Ryan turned 14, I had a suspicion he was going to be gay. In the end, when I found out that he was gay, I was a little bit shocked. At the end of the day he's my son, and of course I'm going to accept him.

Ryan didn't have a lot of friends growing up, and he lost a lot of the people he had through the stages that he went through. But as father and son, we were always close. It was a shame that we fell out when we did. At the time, I was in a difficult relationship, being told what I could and couldn't do. Foolishly, I did as I was told, and I fell out with Ryan because of it. My partner couldn't accept that he was gay. Ryan moved out and set up a flat all on his own.

I dumped her in the finish because I decided I would not lose my son over a relationship. It took us some time, but Ryan and I became close again.

One day, he asked me if I would take him to Southampton for an interview at university. We drove down together. He passed the interview stage, and I moved him down in a van to the students' flat. Ever since he went to university we've been close again.

'I love him to bits, and I'll do anything for him'

To the parents out there, I would say, do as you've always done. Support them as much as you can. Ryan's a wonderful son, and he couldn't have a better partner than Matthew. My advice for parents is to support them and always be there for them. At the end of the day, you'll regret not standing by them because they'll turn the other way. You'll lose them.

As for me and Ryan now, we've made up. I love him to bits, and I'll do anything for him. We're always in contact, even though we live 150 miles apart. I may not understand everything he does, but I love him anyway.

I only know that he's still aiming for the top. What they are achieving now, he's got his head screwed on. They've got plans, he's always one step in front. But he's always looking for different things. He's so creative like that.

'I couldn't be prouder of the son that I've got'

I am so proud of Ryan. My mum idolised him as a little boy. If she knew now – she died ten years ago – what he'd become she would be so so proud of him. He's got his college diploma and then his degree from Southampton University; but, beyond anything else, he went on to get his master's degree. I had tears in my eyes throughout his graduation ceremony. That really meant the world to me.

Ryan has turned out to be a lovely, lovely chap who I can call my son. What he's achieved is beyond me. He doesn't get his brains from me! My brains are in my hands, but Ryan has got it up in his head. He's got an incredible creativity; that's why he's doing so well. He deserves it.

Always let your child do what they think is best. If they need your help, they will come and ask for it. I couldn't be prouder of the son that I've got.

Dear parents: Welcome to 'me'!
COMING OUT TO YOUR PARENTS IS NEVER EASY.

If you are fortunate enough to have parents, or one parent, or carers who love you, that fact alone puts you under pressure. The knowledge that they will almost certainly have expectations of you can add to the stress.

So, part of preparing yourself to tell them might be preparing them. Even the most loving, open, accepting parent can react badly. Sometimes people need time to process and understand, simply due to a lack of knowledge.

The following section is for your parents. You can show this to them if you feel able to.

♡ Parents' guide to LGBTQIA+ coming out

For most young people, even now, coming out can be a watershed moment, a huge release of fear, hope, relief and joy. Either way, approach the subject with sensitivity. Remind them that they can trust you. You might want to give them gentle nudges, but don't blurt out questions – the words should come from them.

If you are surprised or shocked, stay calm and think before you speak. Here are some gentle things you can say in the moment:

- **I'm pleased you told me.** Your child has trusted you with something that they have probably known about all, or most, of their lives. Feel honoured – express that to them and ask them how they're feeling now that they've told you. It gives them, and you, time to process.
- **Can I give you a hug?** Sometimes we don't need words to express our love and acceptance. Even if they say no (maybe they're too overwhelmed for touch), knowing that the offer of physical comfort is there will go a long way.
- **Have you told anybody else?** And if they have – don't be offended. Your child probably used somebody else as a sounding board, as telling a parent can be loaded with baggage and fear. Be reassured that they were smart and open enough to seek help and haven't been going through this alone.
- **Do you need me to tell anyone?** Coming out can be an emotional and exhausting experience, and they might need you to tell the other parent or Grandma.

And these are the things you should either avoid or be careful around saying:

- **I already knew!** Some find it comforting that close friends and family were already aware. Others are horrified and worry you were talking about them behind their back. To be on the safe side, *don't say* you already knew unless they ask you.
- **It's just a phase!** Do NOT say this. To assume heterosexuality or being cisgender is the thing we must aspire to be is downright offensive and hurtful. Any child coming out to you is informing you that *this* is who they are; questioning that is a put-down, whether you mean it to be or not.

Joanna Fortune is a psychotherapist specialising in the parent-child/adolescent relationship. She is also a trauma and attachment repair specialist with over 20 years of clinical experience. We asked her some of the questions that we often get asked by parents:

1. I think my child might be gay. Should I wait for them to talk to me about it first or open up the conversation myself?

As parents, we should focus on creating and holding a safe space within our family homes and also within our relationships with our children for them to question, explore and express themselves, and this includes questioning, exploring and expressing their sexual identity. So, rather than you telling your child that you think they are gay, ensure that you use safe, open language at home and create and nurture an environment of safety and inclusiveness so that they know that they can share this part of their identity with you when they feel ready to do so.

2. My child has come out and I'm totally happy for them, but my partner is struggling with it. How can I support them both?

When we parent our children we do so with an unconditional love. There are no conditions on our love for them. Your partner might be struggling with this part of your child's identity, but the love they share for your child should not be compromised by this. Sometimes we need to be reminded of that fact. Approaching your partner with acceptance and empathy while maintaining a boundary for how they express their difficulties is another part to this, for example, 'I know that this is hard for you. I do not yet know what part of this is proving so hard for you, but I am open to listening and understanding your perspective and I want you to explore and work this out with me and never with our child. It is not our child's responsibility to support you on your journey with this, that is for me and you to work through. We love and accept our child.'

3. I worry my child won't talk to me about their life or is living a double life. They seem completely shut off, and it feels as if we don't bond at all. How can I repair our relationship and encourage them to open up to me?

It is quite normal and even healthy for teenagers to seek increased privacy from parents; they want to keep aspects of their lives away from us and this is part of the developmental task of adolescence to pursue autonomy and independence from us parents. However, privacy seeking is not the same as secrecy. It can be very hard to know that there are parts of our children's lives we are not fully aware of, and this can prompt us to cross that line from being interested in their lives to becoming intrusive in their lives. If we are intrusive, we will only push our teenagers further away from us.

Try to step back, pause, reflect to your teen that you love them and always will. Add that you know they are growing up and will want to keep you out of some parts of their life but that you are always available and interested in hearing about them and their life. Remind them that you are their safe place, and explicitly state that they can talk with you about anything and you will never judge.

Then, each day, ensure that you catch their eye and smile at them, tell them that you love them, offer a hug and, when they speak, ensure that your nose follows your toes – turn your whole body and face towards them to show that you are available and interested in that communication.

When you feel your child pulling away from you, try to avoid demanding that they speak to you and share with you, and instead try to respond with nurture, connection and positive actions. Make their favourite meal or snack and eat that together before joining them on the sofa, and, while sitting in close physical proximity, watch the show they are watching without judging and dismissing it, and be interested in what interests them so they learn that they are interesting to you.

4. I'm so worried that my child will get bullied for being different. How can I protect them?

This is hard for any parent. We desperately want to protect our children from every harm or negative outside influence, and we cannot guarantee that they will never experience the cruelty of others in the world, much as we might try to. We lead by example; we focus on what we can do. We ensure that our children grow up knowing that they are exactly who they are supposed to be, are valued, enjoyed, loved and safe. We challenge negative stereotypes and derogatory language each and any time we hear it, so our children know what is and isn't okay and how to challenge such behaviour in others when they are exposed to it. We teach our kids to be allies and to stand up for themselves and each other. This is the task of parenting: to raise independent, socially minded and engaged adults in the world. Explicitly tell your child that you want them happy and safe and that *if* anyone ever behaves towards them in a way that leaves them feeling unsafe or uncomfortable you want to know about it, you will listen and you will support them and can step in if they ever need you to do so. Sometimes our children and teenagers need to know that we are a safe place for them to emotionally exhale into and that we will listen before jumping in to act. If you feel that your child is being bullied for their sexual identity, this is discrimination and is unacceptable in every single instance. If it happens in school, notify your school and tell them that you want their bullying policy enacted in the first instance.

5. I'm terrified of coming out to my parents and worried they won't accept me for who I am. How can I start the conversation with them?

Open and honest is the best approach. Tell your parents that you have something you want to share with them, but you are really nervous about it and want to handle it in a way that you feel as comfortable as possible with.

Ask them when might be a good time to have a private, uninterrupted conversation. Sometimes our parents seem irritated when really they are distracted, so asking them when is a good time is about creating a safe physical time and space for the conversation. You could do what parents sometimes do when they want to bring a difficult conversation up with their teenagers – wait until you are in the car and while side by side (less intense than face on), tell them that you have something personal to share with them and you can start that conversation now and then take space so you can each reflect on it and set a time to come back together and extend that conversation. It might help you to have a safe support person with you who already knows this about you so that you feel supported in getting the words out. Be open to being surprised by your parents; they may already have an idea about this part of your life; they may be focused only on your happiness.

6. I spoke to my parents about my sexuality, and it didn't go well. I feel they don't get me at all, and I don't know how to start rebuilding our relationship.

Be open and honest always. Tell your parents (verbally or in a message) that the conversation didn't go as you had hoped it would go. Then state how you had hoped it would go: 'I had hoped that you would hear me, hug me and tell me that you love me no matter what and will support me', and wonder with them if you guys might start the conversation over now that they've had time to think about it.

Reassure them that you are happy within your sexual identity, that it is a part of you but not all of you, you are still the same teen you were before you told them this information. All you wanted was to be open and honest with them. Beyond this, you cannot control their response, and I am so sorry that this didn't go as you wanted and as you deserved it to go.

Please ensure that you have people outside your parents with whom you can be honest and feel safe and supported.

Sometimes our tribe is within our family, and sometimes it is outside our family unit. Don't give up on them; let them know that you love them too and want your relationship to improve and are ready to discuss this when they are ready. And lean into your tribe in the meantime.

Being calm, open-minded and supportive to your LGBTQIA+ child is the way to be a Rainbow Superhero.

Top Ten Tips for Parents

1. Listen with an open mind. Your child is experiencing something you might not understand, but that's not always a bad thing.
2. Show an interest in their issues – political and personal. Learn from them about what is important in their world.
3. Ask questions if you don't understand, but try to do this with genuine interest and an open heart.
4. Ask which pronouns they prefer: she/her, he/him, they/them. It might not be your thing but it's theirs, and it will cost you nothing.
5. Mind your own business about sex. No child wants to talk to their parents about that. Just remind them to be safe and that's your job done. But be open to listening to them if they do want to chat, and make it clear you'll always be there for them.
6. Don't get defensive and into arguments or fights with bigots trying to protect them. Fight your kid's corner through positivity and love.
7. Reassure them about the future. Help them build a Rainbow Family, starting with you.
8. Take their side morally. Tell them that bigots and bullies never win, and that you'll always be there to listen, help and understand.
9. Encourage them to be themselves, and bite your tongue when that doesn't fit in with your ideas. ALL kids act out and dress uniquely.

10. Congratulate them for coming out. Tell them that this is a new beginning, the world can be theirs, and you're proud of them.

Let them find their own way.

You can sit in the backseat, but remember they are the ones driving. Just keep being a parent.

You might know or suspect your child is LGBTQIA+ and they might choose not to tell you – and that is okay. The most important thing, always, is that you are their parent and you love them.

It's important to remember that your child is just that – yours. It doesn't matter if they are LGBTQIA+; they are still the same person – your child. It doesn't make any difference in the end.

Matthew and Ryan chat with...

Supermum (or as she calls herself 'Mamma Bear') Felicity Harfin from @harfinfamily

Felicity is one of our closest friends who we met through our joint love of creating content, showing you can meet your best friends online! She is raising her two sons to be open-minded, amazing people. Knowing Felicity has taught us that regardless of your child's orientation and gender, at the end of the day great parenting is simply about love.

M&R: How has sharing your family life online with your sons impacted your relationship with your boys?

Felicity: It actually has a really positive impact because working to create content together means there is a central point every single day when we have to come together to work. Whether we are doing comedy sketches, or blog-style posts or putting up gaming content, we always have to listen to each other. Essentially, we are a working team. It was a dream of my sons to work in social media – three years ago I didn't know how to log onto Facebook! My boys are everything to me, so I gave them my full support and now we are a business as well as a family! I never imagined social media would take off as much as it did, but it has been an extraordinary experience. The boys have had so many fantastic opportunities they would not have had otherwise – to travel, meet their heroes on red carpets. Most importantly, though, they have learned a great work ethic; they really put their heart and soul into this, and it makes me very proud. We have always been close, but there is another layer added when you are working together. I respect them as people, not just as my children. We listen to each other's ideas (they often have better ideas than me!), so working as a team has been really positive for us as a family.

M&R: A lot of parents worry about their children being online too much. Do you have you any tips?

Felicity: Online and social is a full-time parenting job right now! Online is a whole new world, and it comes down to trying to be as open as possible with your kids and keeping it as a two-way street so that they are never afraid to come and talk to you – about anything.

It's my job now, but I didn't grow up around technology and as somebody who works in the field, I can really see how daunting it must be for parents navigating everything that is out there right now. Monitoring is key. We have a strict policy in our house – we sit down for dinner at 8.30 every night, no phones at the table and no gaming after dinner. The boys are used to it – they don't know any other way. One of the positive things about working in social media is that we spend so much time creating content, there is very little time for any of us to sit scrolling. Online is our kids' world right now so there is no way of avoiding it, but it's important to monitor the places they are going and the effect it can have on their moods and well-being. You just have to work out what are the fair restrictions for your child. Protect them but also give them freedom.

M&R: We have shared such great times as part of your family, Felicity. The Disney cruise?

Felicity: What a trip! It was so amazing, and the great thing about you guys is that you have a great work ethic, which is so good for my boys to look up to, but that trip really showed us how much fun we all have together! The way you can suck in all the enjoyment and make the most of life – that's so important.

M&R: We clicked with you straight away when we first met – you were instantly so warm and welcomed us into your lives like family. How important are family/friends to you?

Felicity: So important! I was an only child and am a single mother, but I love gathering people around me. I am a real Mama Bear, loyal and protective. For the boys, it is so important to have other people around them, not just me. You have been such great role models for the boys, invaluable for giving them advice and for them to turn to when they need something I can't give them.

I think it's essential, even if you have a big family, to pick a chosen family, people who are close enough for your kids to ask those embarrassing questions they don't want to ask their parents. Even small things, like that time my boys were having problems styling their hair right? I had no idea how to help them myself, so I rang you guys...

M&R: And we ran over with our gels and waxes to save the day.

Felicity: Hair superheroes – you totally nailed it!

M&R: Lastly Felicity, you have taken your boys to the Pride parade every year since they were babies, right? Explain why Pride means so much to you.

Felicity: They have never missed it. LGBTQIA+ people have always been a part of my life. There has never been any question about accepting or not accepting anyone. When I was 14, my best friend came out to me. But I think that ethic came from when I was very, very young. My grandfather was from an extremely conservative family and was a judge in a

Scottish law court when I was a child. Grandad's best friend was gay, and this was at a time when being homosexual was actually illegal. This family friend was arrested several times, and my grandfather had to keep him out of prison. Because of this background, I had it drilled into me that the world was not equal, and I grew up understanding that prejudice like that was unjust and wrong. That is how I have brought up my boys: to understand how important it is to stand up for what is right. And part of that is standing up to support our friends and be a part of a community that celebrates difference and diversity.

> Supermum quote!
> 'As a parent, I've hopefully raised my family with the idea that their sexuality is exclusively theirs to share or not. Everyone, no matter sex, race, education, religion, dress sense, is human and deserves to be treated and loved in the same way.'

♡ The last word in our 'Parenting' chapter goes to Felicity...

> "The most important thing is to be able to love!"

♡ A Rainbow Family of your own

> *Elton John (singer)*
> The greatest decision I've made – well, we've made – in the last six years, is to have those boys.

One of the things that parents worry most about in having an LGBTQIA+ child is that they won't be able to have grandchildren.

Being parents is definitely part of our life plan, and when the time is right we hope to grow our family for ourselves – and while our parents are still young enough to babysit for us!

Same-gender parents are increasingly visible on TV and in the media, which is so encouraging, and surrogacy and adoption have made same-gender parenting possible – great news for couples like us.

A same-gender married couple we LOVE is Whitney and Megan Bacon-Evans – otherwise known as 'Wegan'. Like us, they are just getting on with their lives as a couple, running their businesses and creating content for @whatwegandidnext. We asked them about their journeys and their extraordinary activism in campaigning for fertility treatment for LGBTQIA+ couples.

♡ Whitney and Megan: Our fertility equality journey

We embarked on our baby journey in 2020 and we thought it was going to be an exciting one, but then we found there was no information or representation for lesbian couples in the system. In fact, we found so many barriers in place that we ultimately realised there was discrimination in place. We were shocked! This was 2020, and we presumed that as we are legally a married couple, we would be viewed as equal to any other family in the eyes of the law. Sadly, it turned out not to be the case.

It all came down to the unfair financial burden being placed on the LGBTQ+ community because we didn't fit the eligibility criteria to receive fertility treatment on the NHS. So, we decided to use our voice and 'influence' for good and launched a petition to raise awareness. In 2021, we launched a landmark test case for equal access to fertility treatment for the LGBTQ+ community.

Then, we spoke in Parliament in January 2022 and in August 2022. We were heard! The government announced their Women's Health Strategy, removing the financial barriers for female same-gender couples to create a family! This is exactly what we hoped to achieve when starting our fight for fertility equality. Our dream of helping create a future where LGBTQ+ families are treated as equal is soon going to be a reality that will positively impact the lives of hundreds of thousands of LGBTQ+ people who can now create a family.

We're still on our own baby journey… so watch this space!

> *Dwayne Wade, former professional basketball player*
> Me and my wife, Gabrielle Union, we are proud parents of a child in the LGBTQ+ community and we're proud allies as well. We take our roles and responsibilities as parents very seriously. So, when our child comes home with a question, when our child comes home with an issue, when our child comes home with anything, it's our job as parents to listen to that to give them the best information that we can, the best feedback that we can, and that doesn't change now that sexuality is involved.

Matthew and Ryan chat with...

Two Dads in London *(@twodadsinLondon)*
Another couple who are raising a family are Super Dads Richard and Lewis from Two Dads in London. We got in touch with them to find out what could lie ahead for us!

M&R: Thank you so much for being a part of our book! Can we start by asking you to give us a quick description of your family and family life?

Richard and Lewis: We are a two-dad family to two children through adoption who are currently seven and four years old. We live in London and always try to have as much fun as possible together. Our days are often filled with all of the usual parenting things that everyone else has to deal with, like packed lunches, the school run and basically not enough sleep, but our weekends are always so busy as we try to fit in so many different experiences together. We love heading out for a ramble in the woods, a walk along the beach or a day pretending to be tourists in London.

M&R: You have two children, so when you went into the adoption process for the *second* time, can you tell us what the most special parts of that journey were for you?

Richard and Lewis: One of the most special moments of the adoption process second time around was asking our son if he would like to have a brother or sister, and he immediately responded with a massive smile to say he wanted a sister. We will always remember this and will talk about it with him and his sister when they are both older. The most rewarding part of going through the process was during the introduction weeks when we got to a point where we had built such a lovely bond with the foster carer, we could see that they were happy knowing we would be parents to the child they had looked after and parented up to that point.

The most heartwarming moment for us was when our son and daughter got to meet and play for the first time ever; it was instant brotherly and sisterly love for them.

M&R: What was the decision to adopt like for you as queer people? There are couples who are having this discussion at home with their partner right now, so can you tell us a bit about what options are out there for them?

Richard and Lewis: It was a very daunting decision for us to make, and at first we were worried about some of the myths that same-gender families can only adopt older children or the harder-to-place children, but once we actually started to go to some adoption events, those worries quickly went away as it was so clear that the need for adoptive parents was huge. Our experience of the process as queer people was excellent, and often we found that some of our own worries were just that – worries of our own and not those of the social workers assessing us. We know that there have been lots of families created through adoption for queer people, but also lots of families created through surrogacy.

M&R: Were there many supports for you when you were starting out? Was there anything in particular you found helpful when you were beginning the process?

Richard and Lewis: There are lots of brilliant charities and groups out there to provide advice and support; one of the best for us was New Family Social, which helps to create long-term links with other families similar to ours after adoption. One of the best pieces of advice we got from the social work team was to avoid reading the forums online as they are often fuelled with the negative experiences people have had, and this can put unnecessary worries in your mind when the truth is that every adoption is completely different, as is becoming a parent in general.

M&R: Can you tell us a bit about your own, personal approach to parenting?

Richard and Lewis: Our approach to parenting is all about balance and remembering that there is no such thing as a perfect parent. As parents, we all make mistakes and that's completely okay; we often don't know all of the answers and will always ask for advice and help from others, but most importantly we try our best to ensure that the kids have a good grounding of being polite, having good manners and understanding that it is nice to be kind. We do have a good balance between us when it comes to parenting as we often split the fun and practical stuff evenly around work commitments to make sure one of us isn't always playing good cop and the other, bad cop.

M&R: Could you describe a few of your biggest challenges early on and how you managed to overcome them as time went on?

Richard and Lewis: One of the biggest challenges for us was constantly adding extra pressure on ourselves to appear as perfect parents. We were always worried that, because we were two dads, we needed to over-compensate. After a while of constantly trying to do this, it hit home that we were putting too much pressure on trying to appear to be perfect parents and that in fact we were not allowing ourselves, and in particular Lewis, to just build a positive attachment with our son. Once Lewis realised this, he arranged to meet with our adoption social worker, and she explained that this is completely normal for lots of new adoptive parents. She put his mind at rest, and it gave him the freedom to not worry so much about the things that are not so important, like forgetting the baby wipes, and instead focus on building the positive relationship as Daddy, and since then we have never looked back. We no longer aim to be perfect parents; instead we always do our best to be the parents that our children need us to be and not what we think everyone else thinks we should be.

> *Anderson Cooper (broadcast journalist)*
> It feels like my life has actually begun, and I sort of wonder, what was I waiting for? This is a new level of love. It's unlike anything I've experienced, and yet it's also very familiar and incredibly special and intimate. It's really extraordinary.

> *Wanda Sykes*
> *(Hollywood actress)*
> Our kids are 12 now, and I am so proud when they're being kind, polite and respectful. But mostly they speak TikTok, so I have no idea what they're saying.

> *Kehlani (singer)*
> All my friends, all her aunties, uncles, her godparents, everybody, is just loudly queer. Our generation already kind of broke the mould in getting to that point, so I don't even think our kids are going to think about it as something that they have to identify and differentiate. I feel it should be normal. We'll be reading queer stories, queer books where the baby has two dads, two moms, two parents who don't identify as either. Watching movies that have that. She sees healthy queer couples. So, I don't think that [my child's] going to even think about it as different from normal.

CHAPTER 8
Love Is Love
Matthew and Ryan's True-Love Story

We get asked questions about our relationship all the time so – finally – here it is: from how we met to where we are today. A peek behind the scenes, including some of our not-so-perfect bits and some embarrassing stuff from our nearest and dearest!

The truth from inside our rainbow relationship starting back at the beginning with…

♡ 101 sprinkles!

Matthew: So, as you know from the beginning of the book, it began with me dressed as an ice lolly! It was such an unromantic start that whenever anyone would ask how we first met, we would just make up a romantic story, like we bumped into each other outside Starbucks and that it was love at first sight, when really we just met because of Tinder. LOL.

Ryan: When Matthew pied off meeting me on Tinder, I made the assumption that he was messing me around and that he was a player, but when he turned up at my work covered in cake sprinkles I could see that he was truly a boss. On Tinder, it's easy to get a false impression of someone, but meeting him face to face we just clicked straight away.

He didn't want to go home or pay for a taxi, so he asked if he could sleep on the couch of my student dorm. But, because I was still annoyed with him, I said no, and he actually ended up sleeping in the train station. I always imagine him – six in the morning, when all the workers were going to work – lying on some bench still in his awful Halloween costume.

Matthew: I was pieing Ryan off because I didn't want a serious relationship at that time. It wasn't that I didn't like him; I just didn't feel very interested in anyone. I also felt unsure at first since Ryan worked in the club. I mean, who wants their partner going to a club where lots of people hook up with each other? But there was something about Ryan that I found so addictive; I knew that I couldn't let him go. I knew that I could trust him, so the worry about his work at the club soon dissolved. And, after Halloween, everything changed.

Ryan: I think that sometimes – through text – conversations and communication get lost very easily. But, after Halloween, we finally arranged a proper date.

♡ The perfect first date

Matthew: I picked Ryan up outside his university house. Naturally, I was in my mini cooper.

Ryan: As I said before, when I first saw Matthew, his car and just the fact that he could drive, I was so impressed. I was a university student and had never dated anyone with a car before – I was so excited!

Matthew: As soon as I picked Ryan up, I was instantly attracted to him, and he was giggly getting in the car, which was really cute. As you already know, we went to Mayflower Park for our first date, but there was something else that happened on that date that we haven't shared with you yet!

Ryan: After the fairground, for some reason I wanted to see how manly Matthew would be in a situation where he had to protect me. Even as I'm writing this, I'm giggling and laughing at myself for how silly and stupid it was. Basically, I asked if he wanted to go and explore a graveyard as once the fireworks had finished it was a creepy dark night.

Originally, he was a little bit scared, but after a bit of persuasion from me he finally said yes and drove us there. The drive was where our connection really grew. It was the first time that I really, truly fell for Matthew. He was super funny; it was like he wasn't even trying to make me laugh, but he just made me laugh by being himself. When we eventually arrived at the graveyard, I wanted to see if he'd get out of the car or if he would be too creeped out. Spoiler alert: he didn't get out of the car because he was too creeped out. Honestly, I thought it was quite charming and endearing.

All joking aside, I really felt like the evening with Matthew had been so special, and it really felt different from any crush

I'd had before. In my previous relationships, trust had always been an issue; always the downfall. But with Matthew, there was absolute honesty right from the start. It was so easy, and there was no drama. I believed fully that he was the one for me, so we both naturally left Tinder without asking and became exclusive. I'm glad that I trusted myself because, many years later, I still feel the same.

♡ Meeting the family

Ryan: During my uni period, I had developed a stronger relationship with my dad. I just told him that I had a new boyfriend and that was it. It would have been a really big deal when I was younger, but, because I had been away at uni and had my independence, I knew that no one but me could have an opinion on my happiness.

Matthew: When I introduced Ryan to my parents it came as a surprise, literally! When he first came back to my house, I didn't directly introduce him because I felt a bit awkward. They knew I'd been staying elsewhere – which was clearly at his house – and I was just being a big wuss, not wanting to have everyone bother me. Looking back, it was ridiculous, but I think I just wanted to keep things nice and simple: to not make anyone feel awkward or to have to mediate between people. My parents were taken aback but remained polite and seemed to like him.

Ryan: I was very excited to meet Matthew's family as he spoke so highly of them, and I knew that he had a great relationship with them.

However, Matthew hadn't told me that they were clueless I was coming round. When we got out of the car, Matthew took me straight to his room. I just followed him and sat on his bed, while his mum was in the kitchen preparing dinner. This made me feel very awkward because she didn't know that I was in the house. It got to the point where it was too late for Matthew to introduce me the way that I thought he would have introduced me. To be fair, I think living with your parents makes things a little bit awkward, especially when you're that age.

At some point, I had to leave the house, and I remember Matthew saying, 'Let's go back and stay at yours.' When I was coming down the stairs, I told Matthew that it was probably best if he sneaked me out, because it was not the most ideal way for me to meet his mother for first time. However, as I came downstairs, she saw me. It was a very awkward first meeting because she had no idea who I was, or even that there was somebody else in the house! Matthew got awkward and a bit shy, and the situation kind of escalated to where it was too late for me to introduce myself without it being even more awkward.

However, around a week later, we had dinner which is where I got to meet his mum and dad together. I got along with them straight away. I'm not gonna blow my own trumpet, but I feel like parents love me anyway because I'm always super polite and I'm usually quite easy to talk to… so I think it went well.

Matthew: No one in my family had really met Ryan before. His first time meeting the rest of my family was at a party – and they loved him! It was such a success, we were dancing, everyone was having a good time, and I was really happy that everyone in the family was embracing my boyfriend. He was even dancing with my mum and my nan! We were all having such a nice time together; that's when I knew that things would get serious, because I knew everyone in my family clearly loved him and approved.

♡ Roscoe – the furbaby

Ryan: A few months after that, it was time for me to move out of my university house. We were in a sticky situation because we hadn't been together for super long, but we also didn't want to live separately, and I didn't want to move in with a random stranger either. So, we took the leap and decided to search for places to live around Southampton.

There were so many awful places we looked at, but we were just excited to have our own space and call ourselves homeowners. It made a lot of sense to move in together because Matthew was spending A LOT of his time at my uni accommodation. I'd say he would stay at mine at least five nights a week. It was almost like he lived with me – however, it would've been nicer to have a place we could call home.

And, of course, we had to get ourselves a dog!

Matthew: Ryan was definitely more into the idea of us getting a place. I was a bit worried because I know that it's expensive and a big responsibility. On top of that, living in a flat with a dog would be a challenge because we were both students and working part time. During the summer, while I was away working for a week, Ryan would not stop harping on about wanting a dog.

Ryan: While Matthew was working – not gonna lie – I didn't listen to him. I carried on looking at dogs: specific breeds that wouldn't bark inside and that could comfortably live within the confines of a flat, which is how I found out about Boston terriers. All along, I was keeping in mind that we wanted a dog to fit our lifestyle, in terms of us being quite active but also being quite lazy – Boston terriers fit that to a tee.

Matthew: When I got back from my week away, Ryan, with a big grin on his face, told me that we were going to London to pick up a dog.

Of course, I was like 'Oh My God! We can't do this!', but, to be honest, he forced me! When we got to London, we picked Roscoe out of a bunch of tiny little Boston terriers. He seemed like the runt of the litter because he didn't seem to be part of the pack. He stole our hearts. I couldn't believe how cute he was; we scooped him up straight away, handed the money to the breeder and went back to our car to head back to Southampton.

We decided on the name Roscoe because at my summer job, someone with the last name Roscoe made a complaint about me. For some reason, I knew straight away that the name was quite special and was perfect for our future dog. Turning a negative into a positive!

My mum said we'd ruined our lives because we wouldn't be able to go on holiday now that we had a dog! Of course, she has since retracted it because she loves Roscoe loads!

Since joining our family, Roscoe has been a huge part of our life and adventures. I can't imagine doing anything without him; he's like our baby, and he fits with our personalities and what we love SO SO SO much!

♡ True love

Ryan: I would joke and say that I was still figuring out if Matthew was the one, but I've known that he was and is from very early on. It was always obvious that he's a caring person because he never tried to change me. Being a guy who wears make-up, I was sometimes judged by my exes, but with Matthew I never had to change who I was. He always accepted that I love to do make-up – in fact, he would encourage me to wear make-up and be myself; he found it attractive for me to be me.

The pinnacle moment – when I realised he was the one for me – was when my mum passed away. In tears, I told him, and he was just there for me. It was about three months into our relationship, and a lot of people wouldn't know how to handle that, but he was my rock; he rose to the occasion completely. It was something that really proved, in my eyes, that he was the one.

Matthew: I was really attracted to Ryan because of the fact that he felt really confident in his make-up. He always says that it gives him confidence and lifts him up. I think, because we were quite young, we both helped each other's confidence without really realising it – be it about how we acted, or what we wanted to pursue in life.

This is something really special that I think a lot of people don't get to experience at such a young age with their partners. Ryan used to have a YouTube channel when we first got together, and every time I was featured, lots of our friends and family would cringe and make negative comments. It made me feel really insecure about trying new things that interested me, like making YouTube videos. But Ryan built up my confidence and helped me to push through – and that's now elevated into a huge online career! We do such incredible things that we experience together as Matthew and Ryan... the brand.

Our Love is Love story ends with a few more moments and memories from our family.

LOVE IS LOVE MOMENT:
Melvyn the tortoise

Matthew had various pets from fish to ferrets. His ferret was called Fluffy, and he later saved up for a tortoise called Melvyn.

Allison Mackinnon, Matthew's mum

LOVE IS LOVE MOMENT:
Crazy golf

Ryan and I always like to have a bit of banter. When I went to Southampton with him and Matthew, we had a game of crazy golf. I was joking with him that I was gonna beat him, and Ryan said, 'You haven't played with me in years Dad. You don't know. I'll surprise you.' Well, he was beating me until the last three holes. Matthew was in second place, I was in last place and then I hit two holes in one and I won it in the finish. I kept teasing him.

Malcolm, Ryan's dad

LOVE IS LOVE MOMENT:
Sister spill

To many, Matthew and Ryan are the kind, caring and happy people we all see online. For me Matthew is the stereotypical annoying younger brother; a part he plays perfectly. Throughout our childhood Matthew thrived on winding me up, something he is yet to grow out of. He loved playing pranks, stealing my chocolates and covering his tracks, telling tales and generally being loud and in your face. Lucky for me most of those irritating habits have been redirected towards Ryan, who is a worthy match for Matthew's mischievous energy. Even luckier, I now have two annoying younger brothers instead of one!

Emma Mackinnon, Matthew's sister

LOVE IS LOVE MOMENT:
101 sprinkles (part 2!)

Around Halloween, for one of mine and Matt's many nights out, Matt decided to dress as a Fab lolly. I went round to his and (at his request) smeared his face with Vaseline and poured sprinkles all over his face. We were laughing so much, and, to make it funnier, no one understood what he was when we were out, but Matt

thought it was such a good outfit. I also think that this was the night he met Ryan!! So now you have the full story!
Stevie Torbica, Matthew's friend

We hope that you have loved reading this book as much as we loved writing it. We believe that is doesn't matter who you love or how you love – love is just love, and that's the most important thing. Even when life and love are confusing, there is always hope. Building a community of like-minded friends to give you the support you need is possible for everyone, but most of all remember to stay true to yourself.

Whatever your gender or orientation: You are unique, you are beautiful, you are YOU!

Letters to Ourselves

Here's what we would have said to our younger selves if we had known then what we knew now.

Dear little Matthew,

I just wanna let you know that when you have those feelings that you don't fit in or when you feel that the little town that you're growing up in isn't where you're meant to be, you are right. And it will all be okay. You have to ride out these next few years at school, and then it will be your time to explore that big wide world you dream about – and boy, it is definitely as amazing as you imagine right now!

You're going to be very anxious about telling people who you really are over the next few years and that you're gay, but if only I could tell you now how amazing it is to come out and how loved and welcomed and accepted you are for being YOU! Concentrate on living in the moment and enjoying everything around you because you have nothing to fear for being you.

There are gonna be some people who call you names and make fun of you throughout your teens, but remember half of them just don't know what it's like to be gay and are in a different mindset. It might feel as if being gay isn't accepted for three parts of your school life, but I promise you it is massively accepted in this big wide world, and there is more to life than the people you're surrounded with at the moment.

Never stop being bubbly, cheeky and pulling pranks on your friends, but the main thing you need to do is have the confidence to stand up for what you believe in. You are amazing, and you don't have to change or be someone else to make other people feel more comfortable.

If you keep that positivity and that cute smile, you're going to have the best life as an open and proud gay man, helping to pave the way for thousands of others like you!

Dear Ryan,

YOU ARE ENOUGH! You don't need validation. Whatever you feel about boys is one hundred per cent completely normal. School is hard, and people don't always understand you. Sometimes you feel isolated and alienated from your peers, BUT know this – there are people like you all over the world, people who feel the same as you. Be yourself. Don't change. Don't lower your voice or hide your hobbies to suit others. Be kinder to yourself. Be patient and gentle and understand that sometimes the people who hurt you must learn from their mistakes to grow and change and be educated. Forgive because people can say and do hurtful things at times, but it doesn't define who they are.

The difficult things you are going through now will make the future you. The attention you don't want now will lead you to a platform that will help others and will allow you to be purely happy with people who love you and understand you for who you truly are.

Surround yourself with people you love and who love you. Have the courage to believe in yourself and lift your dreams. Block out negative people – cruel words are not a reflection of who you are. When you feel as if you've got no one and you're lost in the world, just remember it's gonna make you who you are.

Keep pushing on, and remember that you are loved and that everything will be okay.

Thank you!

Thank you so much for letting us share our stories and our experiences with you, and, from the bottom of our hearts, we hope that your lives as part of the LGBTQIA+ community are as enriching and fulfilling and FUN as ours are! The journey is not always straightforward, but we hope this guide has helped show you that you are not alone and that the most important thing is to just keep being your authentic self and loving yourself for who you are.

After all, no matter *how* you love or *who* you love – Love *Is* Love and that is all that matters.

Finally…
SHINE LIKE A RAINBOW

What the colours of the original Pride flag actually mean and what they mean to *us*.

Red is for life.
LGBTQIA+ people can live full lives with everything they deserve, including families and acceptance.

Orange is for healing.
If the journey is not straightforward, we promise time will heal. You have the support of our community to help you.

Yellow is for sunlight.
The world is changing, and the future is sunny and bright for LGBTQIA+ people and their allies.

Green is for nature.
Who you are and what you are is perfectly natural. Remember those penguins!

Pink is for sex.
Take your time. Trust your attractions, but remember, they may change. Don't be in a rush to define you or your desires.

Turquoise is for magic.
Magic happens when we invite people into our world and share our hopes and dreams with them.

Indigo is for serenity.
When you feel anxious or afraid try to remember that this moment will pass. It takes a lifetime to build a life and you are just beginning.

Violet is for spirit.
Never feel shame. Be your authentic self in the world and your spirit will shine through.

Colours of Progress

Five more colours were added to the original flag as a chevron in 2018: black and brown to represent LGBTQ+ communities of colour, and pink, light blue and white, which are used on the Transgender Pride Flag.

We are all in this together.
Celebrating our Rainbow World.

A Letter from Matthew and Ryan

We would like to say a massive thanks to all of you for picking up this book. Whether you came across it in our social media feeds or in a bookshop, we are *so* grateful to you for taking the time to read something that we have put so much work and love into.

If you liked it and want to keep up with Thread's latest releases, you can sign up here:

www.thread-books.com/sign-up

(Your email will never be shared, and you can unsubscribe at any time.)

We wanted this book to speak to those young people who are worried that their LGBTQIA+ identity will make their life more difficult. The message we wanted to send is that the most important part of you is not your sexuality, or your gender. The most important part of you is just BEING YOU!

Thank you SO much for buying this book, and if you enjoyed it, we hope you might think about writing us a review online. (No pressure – just spreading the word!)

Now you have read the book, we would LOVE to invite you into our online family!

Thanks again!

⬛ matthewandryan

🐦 matthewandryan

📷 matthewandryan/

◼ @matthewandryanuk

▶ @MatthewandRyan

Resources

There is so much help out there – in real life and online. Never be afraid to reach out and ask for help. You are part of a strong, supportive community – all you have to do is reach out.

LGBTQIA+ information and helplines
The Trevor Project
OULGBTQ+ Society
LGBT Foundation
Just Like Us
Switchboard LGBT Helpline

Mental health services
UK Mind LGBTIQ+ mental health
UK LGBT Health & Wellbeing
TikTok Youth Support
New Zealand LGBTQIA+ Support
Australian LGBTQIA+ Support
CANADA LGBTQIA+ SUPPORT
Republic of Ireland LGBTQIA+ Support
USA LGBTQIA+ Support

Pride
News pride.com
International Global Pride Events Calendar

Gender specific
Mermaids: Organisation supporting transgender, non-binary and gender-diverse children, young people and their families.

Gender Rebels Podcast: Weekly question-and-answer podcast that explores life outside the binary. Hosted by Faith, a transgender woman in Brooklyn, and her cis female partner Kath.

Advocate.com: News website and information source for all things LGBTQIA+.

Genderedintelligence.co.uk: Charity dedicated to increasing understanding of gender diversity and improving trans people's quality of life.

Glsen.org: US website championing LGBTQ students, creating school environments free from bullying and harassment.

Genderqueerid.com: Website building awareness, information and resources for genderqueer, non-binary, questioning and gender non-conforming people and their allies.

TV shows – because we deserve to see ourselves represented in all kinds of stories, across every genre
The Umbrella Academy
Pose
Steven Universe
Sex Education
Sense8
She-Ra and the Princesses of Power
First Kill
We're Here
It's a Sin
Will & Grace
RuPaul's Drag Race
Special
Legendary
Schitt's Creek

LGBTQIA+ documentaries that everyone should watch!
Equal [docu-series]
Are You Proud?
Paris Is Burning
The Death and Life of Marsha P. Johnson
Do I Sound Gay?
Disclosure
Tongues United
Olly Alexander: Growing up Gay
Defiance: Voices of a New Generation
Louis Theroux: Transgender Kids
Welcome to Chechnya

> Just Like Us, the LGBT+ young people charity, share their top tips on how you can get involved and contribute to the community:
>
> 1. Want to get involved with the LGBT+ community and take action to improve the lives of LGBT+ young people? You can volunteer with Just Like Us, the LGBT+ young people's charity. Sign up at www.justlikeus.org. You'll be trained to speak in schools about allyship, and you'll make lots of new LGBT+ friends.
> 2. You could also take action at school – is there an LGBT+/ally club? If not, speak to a teacher about setting one up. Just Like Us can help schools set up a Pride Group so that LGBT+ pupils have a safe place to meet in school.

♡ Matthew and Ryan online

Join us and some of our social-media friends:
Whitney and Megan
Cole and Abbie
Søren @supersupersoren
Two Dads in London
Jammi Dodger

Sherbetlemon007
Once Upon a Journey
Our Taste for Life
Harfin Family

Acknowledgements

From the gay couple who started filming videos on their phones in their university bedroom, to AUTHORS?! THIS IS CRAZY! It's safe to say 2015 Matthew and Ryan would be well and truly pooping themselves right now! And we have A LOT of people who have helped make our ideas of *Love Is Love* come into reality.

We want to thank YOU, our incredible online family, for being so open and trusting us in some of your most vulnerable times. You guys supporting us have opened so many incredible doors, and this is one of our ways of saying thank you, and we truly hope this helps you, a friend or a family member. And remember, you will ALWAYS have us to fall back on.

We must say a MASSIVE thank you to Claire Bord for believing in us and supporting this incredible opportunity. We can't thank you enough for all of your advice in helping shape this book to what it is. We hope working with us has been an equal joy – we have genuinely loved working with you and hope to leave something special with you forever: an addiction to BELOW DECK! :P

Nina Winters – OMG you have been the DREAM! You really have helped us get through the rollercoaster that comes with writing a book – and we're sure there were times you wanted to pull your hair out and walk away (it's fine to admit this!! haha), but we can't thank YOU enough for all the patience and time you've given us to help make this book everything it is. We can't wait to meet up for a cuppa and chats over our love for all things anime and Japan.

Morag Prunty, Leona Mullally and Francis Lawrence – you guys are the three amigos with too much creativity and excitement for the world to handle. If we could all sing, it's safe to say we would be the next big girl band of our time lol! What a journey we have had together, and we thank you so much for helping shed light with your understanding and compassion for our stories, and of course many others of those within the LGBTQIA+ community.

Myrto Kalavrezou, Melanie Price and everyone at Bookouture who we may not have directly worked with, but who have made incredible contributions behind the scenes in helping us deliver this book to everyone possible – we owe you SO much thanks.

Marianne Gunn O'Connor – it's absolutely CRAZY that we haven't met you in person, yet without you and your amazing connections and dedication to push us to succeed, this whole book/project wouldn't have happened. We thank YOU for your amazing input and advice, and we are SO excited to finally meet you for that coffee on your next adventure to London!

To those who opened up and contributed to this book by sharing their stories and experiences – we thank you for being so willing, and each and every one of you has made, and will continue to make, a big difference to so many people across the world, for living your best and most authentic selves. We love you guys!

- Felicity – Harfin Family
- Whitney and Megan
- Cole and Abbie
- Supersupersoren
- Two Dads in London
- Jammi Dodger
- Sherbetlemon007
- Once Upon a Journey
- Our Taste for Life
- Joanna Fortune
- Just Like Us – the incredible work you do is already changing and paving the way for our community. You're all an inspiration every day and the most incredible charity we have the pleasure to continue working with.

To our closest friends and family – thank you so much for always supporting us. Through the ups and downs, we do really acknowledge and appreciate EVERYTHING you all do.

www.ingramcontent.com/pod-product-compliance
Lightning Source LLC
Chambersburg PA
CBHW030258100526
44590CB00012B/438